SCIENCE, THEOLOGY
AND EINSTEIN

SCIENCE, THEOLOGY AND EINSTEIN

by

IAIN PAUL

NEW YORK
OXFORD UNIVERSITY PRESS
1982

BL240.2
P3

Library of Congress Cataloging in Publication Data
_____

Paul, Iain.
    Science, theology and Einstein.
    (Theology and scientific culture; 3)
    Bibliography: p.
    Includes index.
    1. Religion and science—1946–
    2. Einstein, Albert, 1879–1955.
    I. Title.   II. Series.
    BL240.2.P3   261.5'5   82–3543
    ISBN 0–19–520378–X   AACR2

Contents

To my dear wife, Liz, and loving children, Findlay and Liza, who served in fuller measure.

General Foreword

The appearance of a series of books on *Theology and Scientific Culture* indicates that we are moving beyond the old antithesis between theology and science, and that the disastrous split in our western culture between the natural and the human sciences is in process of being healed. The increasing pervasiveness of science in our modern life is due not merely to the impact of new technologies on our everyday existence, but to the fact that science has been throwing up integrative modes of thought which have far-reaching implications for knowledge in every sphere of human enterprise. To a unifying outlook of this kind theology has much to offer, as in dialogue with natural science it gains a deeper understanding of the creation through which God makes himself known to mankind. Moreover, it is more and more being realised by natural science through dialogue with theology that empirico-theoretical science as we have developed it owes not a little to the injection of Judaeo-Christian ideas about the universe and its contingent order into the framework of its regulative beliefs.

The day is fast receding when people regarded theology and science as mutually exclusive or when the natural sciences were despised by the humanities as having little to do with the finer and more intangible levels of human life and thought. All sciences, human, natural and theological, share the same concern for the integrity, authenticity and beauty of the universe in which God has placed us, the same passion for objectivity and truth in our mul-tivariable relations with reality, and the same call for humility born of the conviction that the created order manifests a range of intelligibility that we may apprehend only at its comparatively elementary levels. Yet the more deeply we probe into the secrets of the universe, the more we become locked into a dimension of intelligibility that transcends its manifestations in the phenomenal patterns of nature and makes them point indefinitely beyond themselves. As our scientific inquiries press hard upon the boundaries of created reality, we find ourselves grasped by a commanding rationality calling for universal respect and commitment beyond the limits of our scientific experience and formalisable knowledge. As the universe unfolds the simplicity, harmony and subtlety of its order to our questioning, the more it is heard to cry out for its Creator. Thus theological and scientific inquiry have begun to overlap and bear upon each other at decisive points. We have entered upon a new age in which we are compelled to reject the old dualisms, change our received notions, and develop richer, unifying forms of thought, more adequate to an enlarged apprehension of the nature of the universe and its transcendent Creator.

The theologians and scientists who contribute to this series are all very different in training and oulook and in religious persuasion. But they all share the same concern to bridge the gap between theology and science and to find ways of developing dialogue between them on a constructive basis. There are no overall directives. Each contributor has been invited to take his own way, so that none is committed to the views of another through sharing in the same enterprise. It is to be hoped that in this way an open and fruitful dialogue will emerge in which many others beyond the immediate contributors to this series will take part.

The Rev. Dr Iain Paul who gives us this very readable volume on *Science, Theology and Einstein* has brought to its writing not only a double training in science and theology, but some thirteen years of research and lecturing in Universities in England and six years of work as a parish minister in Scotland. His training and experience have forced him to wrestle with the nature of rigorous scientific thinking not only in pure science but in Christian theology as well. Moreover, in preparing this work he spent a year at Princeton steeping himself in the work of Einstein and coming to terms with his epistemological foundations. The contribution which Dr Paul has offered us comes from deep within the intellectual activity of both sides of the discussion, and will do much to reinforce the bonds that are steadily being forged between theological and scientific culture.

Thomas F. Torrance

Preface

Many Christians today share the view that the scientific enterprise and Christian faith are radically opposed to each other. Albert Einstein died in 1955 having achieved world fame as the foremost scientist of the twentieth century. This essay is an attempt to persuade Christians that Einstein has something distinctive and worthwhile to offer to them. This becomes strikingly apparent even when his comments on scientific research are compared with the most rudimentary notions of Christian theology. In the light of his contributions, vast areas of mutual interest are briefly illuminated. Indeed, Einstein has set the stage for contemporary discussions of the relation of science and theology by communicating that sense of action which is scientific research.

Once modern science is apprehended in terms of the openness and realism explained by Einstein, Christians can penetrate to the hospitable reality behind the hostile appearances of modern scientific endeavours. They can place themselves in a much better position to curb anti-scientific or anti-Christian bias and to contribute to the on-going dialogue between modern science and Christian theology.

Several inveterate attitudes to modern science are discussed before raising the question, "Why think scientifically?", as the initial step toward an understanding of science. Some popular misconceptions are considered. The relevance of Albert Einstein's writings is indicated, followed by a description of the personal dilemma of the scientific researcher. Einstein's insights on the role of experience in the origin of scientific concepts and their function in ordering experience are presented. His outline of the advancement of scientific theories is given. Einstein's ideas are illustrated using his assessment of Johannes Kepler's contribution. Next, the importance of the intuitive relation is stressed and the tension between the logical and creative elements of scientific thinking is discussed.

Possible theological connections with Einstein's metaphysical framework for scientific research are faintly drawn before giving reasons for sketching the development of one brief phase of his researches. The contents of his four scientific papers published in *Annalen der Physik* in 1905 show the importance of scientific continuity and industry. Scientific commitment, action and freedom are considered in the context of Einstein's religious views. An assessment of his article on the mechanics of Newton underscores the consistency of his thinking and prepares the way for a discussion of various forms of subversive superficiality in Christian thinking. Differences in everyday, technological and scientific thinking are outlined as a prelude to a detailed examination of Rudolf Bultmann's defense of demythologism.

A comparison of Einstein's epistemological utterances and his four papers represents an attempt to understand basic aspects of modern scientific thinking. Some events associated with those papers are also considered. His thoughts on the relation between science and religion are given before answering the question, "Why think scientifically?", from an Einsteinian perspective of openness and justification.

It is hoped that the partial and inadequate views presented in this essay will be corrected and enriched by Christian thinkers and scientific researchers. It is with such tentativeness that this contribution is offered. Both scientific research and Christian theology have taught the author that even to fail in what is undoubtedly a great and exciting task is to make the path easier for the much more capable who follow.

I should like to express my indebtedness to my patrons, the Trustees of the Center of Theological Inquiry, Princeton, and to Dr L. Charles Willard and the staff of the Robert E. Speer Library, who made the writing of this essay so agreeably possible. My debts to the Reverend Dr James I. McCord, Chairman, the Center of Theological Inquiry, and President and Professor of Theology, Princeton Theological Seminary, and to the Very Reverend Dr Thomas F. Torrance, Emeritus Professor of Christian Dogmatics, University of Edinburgh, for their sensitive encouragement and inexhaustible kindness cannot be adequately expressed in words.

I should like also very specially to thank the Reverend Dr S. W. Peat with whom I have been privileged to travel over many years along the pathways of science and theology, the Reverend W. Haisley Moore whose unselfishness, enthusiasm and industry enabled me to accept the leave of absence generously granted by the Presbytery of Hamilton and accommodated by the congregation of Craigneuk and Belhaven Parish Church, Church of Scotland, and Jean (Mrs Alexander) Steele who prepared the typescript accurately, swiftly and cheerfully.

Iain Paul.

1. QUESTIONABLE INTRODUCTIONS

Scientists with more than a passing interest in theology are often asked by fellow Christians, "Are you capable of overcoming your scientific way of thinking?"[1] This question can be understood as a challenge to the possible assumption that theology is scientific. It can also represent an ingenuous request for an explanation of how modern science relates to theology. On the one hand, those scientific researchers are faced with an Augean task of accepting the challenge of Christians who know very little about scientific thinking. On the other hand, they are invited to precognize what can only be partially realised after the initial theological quest. Little is gained by evading a question which its propounder has already decided is easily answerable. In short, scientists studying theology are soon caught in an Einsteinian dilemma of compulsory exposure to the prior commitments of a (Christian) reporter.[2]

Unfortunately, this kind of introduction is only a small piece of a very large puzzle. No doubt within their own professions many Christians perform, for the most part, as gifted, informed and wise persons. But when it comes to modern science and its methodologies, their conversations, orations and publications show frequently a blatant disregard of professional standards. A considerable ignorance of the complexities of current scientific research is poorly concealed by an incredible confidence in its consequent deficient understanding of modern science. Without themselves having read, let alone graduated or researched, in the natural sciences many Christians write about and critically comment on modern science. Some of the same experience-shy discoursers then demand of scientific researchers what amounts to a vocational capitulation before they are allowed to *read* theology as a responsible approach to creative dialogue. The basic problem seems to be that many Christians weigh modern science and scientists on heavily tilted balances.

To appropriate the words of the physicist Gerald Holton, relatively few Christians "have faced the real magnitude of the problem, or are aware of the large range and amount of scientific knowledge that is needed before one can 'know science' in any sense at all."[3] In some instances, the telling retort of Thomas H. Huxley is still relevant. "If there were an ancestor whom I should feel shame in recalling it would be a man of restless and versatile intellect who, not content with success in his own sphere of activity, plunges into scientific questions with which he has no real acquaintance, only to obscure them by aimless rhetoric and distract the attention of his hearers from the point at issue by digressions and appeals to religious prejudice."[4]

In particular, a powerfully confusing cocktail is virtually guaranteed if elements from philosophies, histories and researches of modern science are arbitrarily mixed. Another common method of clouding the issue is to equate the experiences of graduates of science, scientific researchers and technologists. Those inventions hamper severely communication among Christians and scientists. Besides, the latter cannot hope to deal with the plethora of resulting problems while introducing themselves to Christian theology. Perhaps understandably, as students of theology they are inexorably reduced to silence on those matters. The overwhelming combination of an acute thirst for theological wisdom and the inescapable vulnerability of their probing questions to misinterpretation accelerates this process. For example, persistent inquiries by a scientist can be easily construed as manifestations of a deep-seated antagonism. Other popular evasions treat them as proof of an inability to appreciate their own scientific experiences, as confirmation of their unsuitability for theological studies or simply as inarticulation. To parallel Einstein's observation, the scientist is suspect in the eyes of the Christian customs officer.[5] Fortunately not all Christians see their role as customs officers.

Nevertheless, the majority of theological students with scientific experience stifle their relevant questions. It is particularly difficult to survive prolonged exposure to such inhospitable conceptual climates. Some of those students compartmentalize their knowledge deliberately. Others dissociate themselves slowly from theological or scientific modes of thought. Many lose irretrievably all desire to engage in constructive dialogue between science and theology. The proof of the pudding is in the eating. Traditionally, studies of the relation between science and Christian theology have largely been left either to Christians lacking scientific wisdom or to scientists with inadequate theologies. More contributions on science and theology are urgently required from Christians who have experience in both the parish church and the scientific laboratory. The following brief discussions of several habitual attitudes to modern science and some popular misconceptions about scientific thinking illustrate that most imperative need.

2. INVETERATE HABITS AND ROUTINE RESPONSES

The Christian Churches must remember the degree to which the inertia of the powerless within their files makes possible the dynamics of the powerful over their ranks. The scales of valuation need to be replaced, not recalibrated. Otherwise the Churches will remain vulnerable to the justifiable charge that they have not taken seriously, or have taken seriously and still misunderstand, the essential nature of modern scientific thinking. As things stand, the Christian Churches are major contributors to the present pervasive ecological pessimism and cultural disenchantment. Their faulty contacts with science and technology impede the flow of Christian stewardship in both society and industry. Exactly how modern Churchmen face this charge is necessarily a matter of personality. It is also of considerable academic, social and ecclesiastical complexity. Sweeping it under a cloak of quasi-authority will not make it go away. Such a response will not render Christians respectable, responsible or intelligible. Such all-too-prevalent and all-too-easy reactions are plainly superstitious. In the best interests of both theology and science, and therefore of society and industry, they should be eliminated as soon as possible.

At one level it is the old story of conflict. Science and its discoveries arising out of the empirical investigation of the world apparently threaten theology, particularly its heterogeneous teaching on such matters as the origin of humankind, its place in the universe and its world picture.[6] Granted, many Christian thinkers have paradoxically abandoned fundamentalism and literalism for de-mythologism as a formal response to the concrete contents of modern science. This movement does not, however, solve basic problems. Indeed, it seems to multiply and obscure them as will be discussed in a later section of this essay.

Sheltered behind a precarious pretext of freedom of thought, many Christian scholars visit their own insecurities and insularities on others, either intentionally or unwittingly. Just as a person's dilated pupils can alert the trained eye to a dangerous habit, so a Churchman's cultivated college can exhibit symptoms of severe addiction to several popular theological hallucinogens. A habit of confrontation has many threads, but the still-lingering tendency among Christians to point to problems which science cannot presently solve is perhaps the most worn. Forty years ago, Albert Einstein commented on the now-familiar fallacy of the God-of-the-gaps. He acknowledged that "the doctrine of a personal God interfering with natural events could never be *refuted*, in the real sense, by science, for this doctrine can always take refuge in those domains in which scientific knowledge has not yet been able to set foot."[7] But he also observed that "a doctrine which is able to maintain itself not in clear light, but only in the dark, will of necessity lose its effect on mankind, with incalculable harm to human progress."[7]

To base any argument primarily on a guess about what science cannot do in a particular age or period is clearly to build on shifting sand.[8] Few scientists, let alone Christians, are in a position to assess what modern science can do. The explanation is simple. Science is not a self-contained enterprise with sharply delimited scope and purpose. Scientific researchers have discovered such vast continents of natural order that the lifetime of a scientist is not long enough to allow him to explore more than one valley. As far as the continent is concerned, he can only hope to read of the adventures of a few of the many kindred spirits. A very popular caricature of science depicts it as the pursuit of humankind's self-alienation from God the Creator. Its popularity depends on the ambiguities created by omitting the multidimensional cultural context which would assist a more realistic identification of both science and scientists.[9] Of course, Christians should not be condemned for their ignorance of scientific research, only for their uniformed criticisms of modern science.

The habit of fear is displayed by a considerable number of Christians. It is weaved principally from the yarn of science as a species of knowledge which dehumanizes humankind, pollutes their planet, and threatens their very survival.[10] Rich with ever-ripe tempting fruit, the tree of science is considered by them as a virulent modern variant of the tree of knowledge of good and evil. With its servile scientists the former needs no seducing serpent.

However, "a sense of cosmic danger is a totally different thing from a tragic sense of life."[11] This vital distinction is more liable to be missed by those who do not take the trouble to weigh carefully the merits of modern science. It can hardly be denied that the discoveries of science lend themselves frequently to exploitation through technology.[10] Technology supplies pesticides, vaccines, nerve gases, nuclear reactors and weapons, medical and industrial instrumentation and so much more. Their immediate appeal often conceals dangerous and addictive properties. Indeed, over thirty five years ago, Einstein realised that "economic and technological developments have highly intensified the struggle for existence, greatly to the detriment of the free development of the individual . . . A planned division of labour is becoming more and more of a crying necessity . . . the spare time and energy which the individual will have at his disposal can be turned to the development of his personality."[12]

Einstein's words exude an optimism and relevance that have proved their durability with the passage of time and the ravages of modern warfare. They also show that the poignant realism of a great scientific thinker acts as an effective personal antedote to the fears of a technologically burgeoning society. Modern science gains a general awareness of the fragility of life. It does not espouse pessimism. Certainly there is cause for careful concern, but not for fear of science. In any case, as the distinguished physicist Max Born warned over a quarter of a century ago, " . . . fear is a bad foundation for reconciliation and solution of conflicts."[13] Reconciliation through apprehension is infinitely superior to dialogue through fear.

It is imperative that the Christian Churches recognise and communicate to their members the relatively confined current role of science in the total cultural metabolism. The fiction of dominant science providing the only intellectually acceptable view of the world is more the product of the non-scientific imagination than the conviction of the research scientist. Besides, as Holton first pointed out twenty years ago, of the vast numbers of graduates of science and engineering in the United States of America a generous guestimate is that about two percent are responsible for the major portion of scientific research.[14] Although the mass media give the impression of being genuinely concerned with science, the newspapers and radio and television stations provide possibly five percent of their space and time for distinctly factual presentation of science.[14] Basic scientific research probably has a share of only a few percent of the total annual expenditure for research and development in the United States of America.[14] There is little reason to assume that the present state of affairs in the Western world is appreciably different.

In other words, all the noise about the threats of science to civilization amounts to the interfering echoes of an ignorance of the contemporary role of science. Such disturbances increase the grave risk of misinterpretation of informative cultural signals. The pursuit of science and scientific thinking provide important reactions that slowly, almost imperceptibly, shift the principal technological, economic, political, ethical and religious equilibria already dominant in the overall system of cultural values.[15] Even within the scientific enterprise reaction rates are hardly impressive. Contrary to popular non-scientific opinion, scientific thought is notoriously conservative when it comes to the assimilation of new knowledge. Recurrently throughout science's history the profoundly original contribution was received with great suspicion.[16]

Two extremely significant recent examples of scientific conservatism were cited by Born, who was awarded the Nobel Prize for his contributions to quantum theory. "The physical world received the suggestion (that finite quanta of energy E exist which are proportional to the frequency v, $E = hv$) with great scepticism as it did not fit at all into the well established wave theory of light. Years passed without much happening. But in 1905 Einstein took up Planck's idea, and gave it a new turn."[17] Born also recalled that Einstein's special theory of relativity, published that same year, needed an effort to assimilate, and that "not everybody was able or willing to do so. Thus the period after Einstein's discovery was full of controversy, sometimes of bitter strife."[18] "Indeed, it was through Minkowski's semi-popular lecture, 'Space and Time' on 21 September, 1908 at the eighteenth meeting of the Naturforscherversammlung, that a number of scientists first became intrigued with relativity."[19] Scientists are characteristically wary of digging theoretical pits lest they should turn out to be intellectual prisons.

The eminent cosmologist Hermann Bondi also stressed the conceptual inertia of scientists. The basic instincts of a scientist, according to Bondi, rebel against the case of a theory that has been extensively tested and repeatedly confirmed over a long period of time and by a large expanse of empirical knowledge, and then is found wanting.[20] The refinement of measurement and the deepening of apprehension may assist in uncovering its limitations. It does not necessarily follow, however, that they will demonstrate its inadequacy within the context in which it was established. The old theory will not yield readily to a new superior rival "that does not diminish the utility of continuing to employ, in a restricted way, a method that has been well tested."[21]

Science increases knowledge. However useless it appears, that knowledge can have its applications which arise often in surprising ways. No one can foresee what those uses may be. Indeed, great caution must be exercised in any application of scientific knowledge, for it is equally difficult to tell from which direction harmful side effects will come. But the intrinsically non-exploitative value of science should not be in question. What now merit critical re-evaluation are the technological uses of scientific knowledge by vested interests through applied "scientists" and engineers serving industry and government.[22] A realistic appreciation of modern science and scientific thinking can only enhance the outcome of such investigations. Of course, it is convenient, even fashionable, to blame science instead of scrutinizing the competitive pressures within industry and examining the military and political priorities of governmental agencies. Ironically, humankind can now send safely three persons five hundred thousand miles on a round trip to the moon. It has still to tackle many of the more immediate problems of dealing with five hundred thousand people travelling only three miles daily to and from their places of employment.[23]

Even the interpretation of the cosmos and the person by technological modes of human behaviour is not the prerogative of the modern scientific thinker. Thus, another cosmologist, W. J. Kaufmann III, wrote, "Only recently have we become fully aware of the ingenuity and depth of insight possessed by ancient peoples in the field of astronomy. The pyramids of Egypt, Stonehenge in England, and the ziggurats of Babylonia are impressive astronomical monuments. In studying these monuments, we realise that for ancient man to have constructed Stonehenge is no less of an achievement than for modern man to have journeyed to the moon. As far back as 3,000 and 4,000 years ago, people had devised elaborate systems by which the motion of the sun, moon and planets could be predicted . . . The systems devised by the ancients for calculating the positions of celestial objects and explaining their motions are truly impressive."[24]

Many Christians presumably know from biblical, archaeological and philosophical sources that technological accomplishments preceded modern science by thousands of years. It is common knowledge that anthropologists have traced the significance of early "industry" back through hundreds of thousands of years. Interestingly, the Yahwistic pericopes of the so-called primeval prologue of Genesis appear to many scientists to bear sustained witness to the importance and abuses of technological innovations within the much broader context of cultural evolution. Evidently, threats of extinction and ecological disaster are not strangers to the people of

God. Indeed, the biblical traditions can be consistently interpreted as the wonderful story of the repeated guidance and deliverance of a faithful remnant from the brink of genocide, the deluge of ecological disaster, and the fetters of technological captivity.

A habit of doom is not the appropriate apparel for a cordial approach to either biblical sources or modern science. Yet some Churchmen approach science and scientists in this very fashion. Contrary to the intrinsic hope of both scientific and Christian thinking, this attitude of doom is commonly based on the abject assumption that humanity cannot be trusted with scientific knowledge. The people who nurse this negativism argue pessimistically that, because of humankind's lust for power, humanity will bring upon itself the ultimate catastrophe unless the triumphal manipulative march of science can be arrested.[25]

Behind such demands for what amounts to a moratorium on science lie at least two fundamental misconceptions. To adapt Holton's insights, one is scientific and the other is theological. First, research scientists do not regard their activities merely as a suitable form of employment.[25] With very few exceptions their researchers are the enactment of their creative thoughts and statements about reality. They regard their activities as small parts of that reality. They relate to the universe as apprehension progressively awakens within them. It is impossible to guard the tree of scientific knowledge so well that no scientist can pick its fruit. Like the hen that crossed the road, scientists get to the other side of a scientific theory. Consequently, it is extremely improbable that Christians will ever arrest the advance of science. At most, they might hinder its immediate progress.

Second, research scientists have been given talents like every person according to his several abilities. If scientists were to choose to bury them on the advice of fellow servants, who cannot properly assess the available options, what would the Lord say to them on returning from the far country? Surely Christians should respect the gifts of scientists, and encourage them to remain faithful over what is truly only a few things. Christians could take a leaf out of one of Einstein's books. Like many scientists, Einstein valued highly the great diversity of human talents, "In order to be content, men must also have the possibility of developing their intellectual and artistic powers to whatever extent accords with their personal characteristics and abilities."[26]

Notably, Einstein's observations cover the much maligned technologists who have long been the subjects of cultural conspiracies. Technologists have to operate within modern societies which have inherited the Grecian and Roman aversion to the use of the hands. Irresponsibly, those societies welcome the proliferation of electrical gadgetry and call for the conservation of energy. Technologists will require cooperation rather than condemnation, if their intellectual gifts are to guide their powerful hands to the cultural plough rather than the commercial sword. Modern societies have yet to implement the belief that all types of human activity are worthy of study and reverence because their pursuit and consequences can enrich or endanger the human condition. Until they do they will continue to squander valuable technological opportunities. The talents of technologists will require careful investment if they are to survive the whims of fickle financiers, the unreliability of skilled workmanship and the inflexibility of industrial management.

Technologists are presently in bondage to big-business. They are also sport on the rack of guilt-ridden social wrath. Ludicrously, the multinational corporation has greater "personal" freedom than the individual technologist. But their oppressors are not confined to private enterprise. For example, medical practitioners have long been heavily dependent on applied chemists, biologists and physicists. Shamelessly, technological consultants are seen, if at all, as the modern equivalents of barber surgeons. It would appear that many Christians are conspirators in an unjustifiable devaluation of the technologist's talents. Indeed, many people who are neither scientists nor technologists are probably more practised in the dark arts of social and industrial manipulation.

The emancipation of technologists could assist the sorely needed, equitable global sharing of precious natural resources. It could nurture the long-overdue caring for the unique cultural heritages of developing countries, and foster the urgently required daring to learn from and cooperate with the long-suffering, badly abused, under-developed nations of this small-minded world. In short, liberated technology could be given the opportunity to attain reflectively and critically determined ends for humankind without the intrusion of false messianic attitudes.

The prevalence of those inveterate habits in the Christian Churches and, therefore, in society and industry, is a major source of alienation between science and theology. In this so-called scientific age, both the person in the street and almost all of the Church leaders and theologians know, at most, very little about modern scientific thinking.[27] Many histories of science, however, point unambiguously to the conclusion that science provides the means for both a vital mechanism for cultural change and an aid to an apprehension of that change.[15]

Scientific thinking is important as part of the total response of humankind to God's Creation. Its restoration to a proper reciprocal contact with theology and a reconciliation of both with the cultural, and therefore spiritual, concerns of all persons are great hopes that can be shared by faithful Christians and committed scientists. Working alongside one another they can discover the mutual benefits of the responsible investment of their God-given talents.[3] Still, considerable difficulties have to be faced before such talk of larger visions can be anchored in reality. Unfortunately, the first step towards an understanding of modern scientific thinking is seldom taken by Christians.

3. THE IGNORED PRELIMINARY QUESTION

The situation is vastly more complicated than the preceding, now-perennial themes would suggest. Available philosophies and histories of science correctly alert interested non-scientists to the existence of philosophical presuppositions that are often tacitly held by scientists. Unless balancing scientific accounts are also consulted, Christians will tend to regard practising scientists as philosophically blinkered, if not blind. As will become evident, such distortions contain a vein of validity, but its motherlode runs deep. The contributions of Ostwald, Mach, Hertz, Boltzmann, Planck, Poincaré, Duhem, Einstein, and many other scientists provide ample evidence of its depth. Nevertheless, ill-informed depreciative attitudes on the part of Christians can only frustrate communication with scientists.

Almost invariably such attitudes are based on inadequate conceptions of both methods at work in contemporary science and topical discussions among scientists themselves. To make matters worse, similar views are actually presented, according to Ernest Nagel, by some philosophers and historians of science. Their "accounts of scientific procedures and interpretations of scientific findings in effect deny both that a scientific theory is ever adopted in the light of a rational evaluation of the evidence, and that the validity of cognitive claims in the sciences is invariant, despite differences in social and personal outlook."[28]

Such scant first-hand knowledge of the procedural diversity of modern scientific research undermines the Christian's confidence in the warranty of scientific methods. It may also entrench the conviction that scientific thinking cannot achieve valid knowledge or evaluate the cognitive worth of its own intellectual products.[28] Perhaps if Christians are made aware of the many obstacles confronting the practising scientist, they will not undervalue, misrepresent, or dismiss scientific thinking so readily.

To anticipate subsequent sections, "there is no *a priori* formula for determining what strategies of research will turn out to be effective"[29] in any given context. "There is no method for judging the comparative merits of competing hypotheses in the light of the available evidence for them."[30] Moreover, observational terms and statements are theory-laden.[31] They are only three of the diverse difficulties with which scientists cope as they tackle the immediate theoretical and experimental problems relevant to their current investigations. If Christians can be persuaded that science exceeds the sum of all its methods and transcends its articulated content, they might reconsider the merits and diversity of scientific thinking.

The father of modern atomic theory, Niels Bohr, enjoyed telling the story of the young scientist who had a horseshoe hanging on the door of his laboratory. His surprised colleagues were unable to contain their curiosity. They asked whether he believed that it would bring luck to his experiments. The young scientist explained, "No, I don't believe in superstitions. But I have been assured that it works even if you don't believe in it."[32] Despite religious prejudice, science works. Besides, superstition would be drastically reduced were more Christians willing to learn of the distinctive features of modern scientific research. The latter are too often believed to be prescribed by current philosophies and histories of science.

For the moment, it is simply stated that scientific thinking cannot be defined by a specific philosophy of science nor confined to a particular history of science. Those points will be referred to later in the text. Granted their validity, the Christian's question, "Are you capable of overcoming your scientific way of thinking," can be seen in a different light. It can be understood as an invitation to describe some of the major hurdles encountered as one pursues both a scientific discipline and the study of Christian theology. Scientists can readily respond to this request, since an explanation must include or presuppose an acceptable answer to the question, "Why think scientifically?" This question requires an answer based on an outline of scientific thinking. Clearly, even at a very early stage in their theological studies, scientists can contribute a partially illuminating reply, given, of course, the proper circumstances. In fact, they are seldom so fortunate. Few Christians show any interest in this preliminary question.

The issue of the relation between modern science and Christian theology is as old as modern science itself. Both traditionally and currently, four basic strategies seem to have been adopted. First, science and theology are independent disciplines, with science addressing the physical domain and theology the spiritual and moral realms. Second, each discipline rejects the other. Many scientists dismiss theology as a sophisticated form of superstition, while a large number of Christians oppose science as a species of heresy. Third, theologies are modified to conform to modern scientific knowledge, apparently reducing conflict. Fourth, the metaphysical aspects of science are accentuated in attempts to increase the interface of science and theology. Surely a sensible strategy must be informed by some notion of scientific thinking together with a compatible answer to the question, "Why think scientifically?" Again, the need to raise this question in this connection is rarely acknowledged by Christians. The preliminary question in any inquiry must be correctly answered if valid answers to all the other questions are to be found.

Many Christians are wisely reluctant to give credence automatically to the utterances of anyone with a scientific background. Presumably the same powers of discrimination should predispose them to read and to learn of scientific thinking from scientists of outstanding ability, accomplishment and articulation. This essay attempts the formidable task of answering the apparently simple preliminary question, "Why think scientifically?" It draws heavily on the published thoughts and works of eminent scientists, but primarily on those of Albert Einstein. Even if its particular perspective proves problematic, it may still activate more gifted Christians with scientific qualifications and experience. If it encourages even one or two to develop, rather than to emaciate, a special interest in the scientific and technological talents of persons for the sake of our Lord, it will have been well worth the effort.

To borrow freely and intensively from the recent essay by Harold I. Brown,[1] this preliminary question, "Why think scientifically?" can be understood in at least two ways. It can be taken as a request for an explanation of why scientists should think scientifically, given that it is agreed that they should think scientifically. It can also be interpreted as a challenge to the common assumption that they should think scientifically which, to avoid begging the question, must be answered without making any assumptions as to whether they ought to think scientifically. No doubt the latter has greater appeal to Christians because it does not limit them to scientific replies. However, it involves the additional difficulties of attempting to evaluate non-scientific responses to scientific apprehension. In fact, many Christians fail or simply refuse to recognise the existence of such problems. Those difficulties are never far from the minds of scientists. They can recall so easily their own painful experiences of learning how to grasp the right end of the research stick. Consequently, they are liable to ask of Churchmen, philosophers and historians what credentials and justifications they think they have for describing scientific apprehension.

The second version is certainly more fundamental. It is intimately related to theology, but it must presuppose some understanding of scientific thinking. It is more sensible, therefore, to begin with the relatively simpler first version. In any case, even a negative answer to it can serve as a reasonable preparation for tackling an acceptable answer to the second version. Of course, Christians can always avoid the issue by simply ignoring this preliminary question, and many do just that.

Without a clear notion of what scientific thinking is, no explanation can be given why scientists should think scientifically. Obviously, the nature of scientific thinking must be the immediate topic of discussion. However, granted the presupposition that scientists should be scientific in their thinking, only scientific answers to this question are acceptable from them. A failure on their part to provide such an explanation why they ought to think scientifically will obviously count against this initial assumption. Their responses must meet any tests for scientific thought that they develop as they attempt to answer this question. But their first concern is to shed some light on what it is to think scientifically. The initial step in every scientific investigation is to prepare the bench by removing recognized obastacles. An analogous preparation will now be attempted.

4. POPULAR SCIENTIFIC FICTIONS

As already indicated, philosophies and histories of science are frequently at variance with the practice of scientists. Actually a large number of scientists remain unaware of those circumstances, while others have merely committed them to memory. When they encounter the inquisitive Christian, however, they are often informed or sharply reminded of harsh reality. This shock treatment also exposes them to the great popularity of a simplistic fiction among Christians. There is a widespread belief that modern scientists are typically proponents of some rudimentary version of Francis Bacon's seventeenth century description of scientific method.[33]

Seen through the eyes of Bryan Magee, this common misrepresentation has the following general content.[34] Apparently scientists believe that researchers experiment under carefully controlled conditions. They measure meticulously their observations, and record systematically their findings. They share their accumulated data with fellow scientists by publishing them in an appropriate form. As the published observations multiply, it is presumed that they recognise general features. Using the latter, they formulate hypotheses that causally relate and embrace all the available data. Next, they test those hypotheses by seeking further observational and experimental confirmations. Supposedly scientists believe that when they succeed in verifying the hypotheses they advance the frontiers of scientific knowledge by discovering new fields of investigation. Last but not least, scientific statements, being based on observational and experimental evidence, are facts that alone represent for scientists absolutely certain knowledge.

It is not a question of Christians deliberately setting up the modern scientist as a straw-man just for the pleasure of knocking him down. In their own undergraduate studies many Christians learned from philosophers that the method of basing general statements on the accumulated observations of specific instances or events is known as induction. They also realised that, according to a very popular view of science, it is the inductive method which distinguishes science from non-science. The same philosophers taught them that David Hume pointed out long ago that no number, however large, of singular observational statements could logically entail an unqualified general statement.

The whole of science is apparently based on an independent

para #3

logical principle (induction) which is incapable of being inferred either from experience or from other logical principles. Consequently, the scientists' talk of facts and their great confidence in the results of scientific research rest uneasily with many thoughtful Christians. The scientists' relative lack of interest in philosophical and historical subtleties only aggravates the situation. In the absence or exclusion of constructive dialogue, Christians often conclude that modern scientists believe foolishly that they attain absolute truth and certainty within the above Baconian framework or its like. It is also frequently assumed that scientific researchers swallow the Baconian exaggeration of factuality but strain at explanation and critical reflection.[33] A commonly associated assumption is that scientists are more amenable to the exploitation of their knowledge than to its cultivation. Or, in extreme form, scientists practise the subjugation of the natural order, while preaching its investigation.

More enlightened Christians can point to abundant documented evidence to show that, at least until the latter part of the nineteenth century, scientists themselves thought and wrote generally but diversely in terms of a single scientific method.[35] Unquestionably, a prominent thread in the procedural web was the description of the pursuit of science given by Isaac Newton. The views of the world's most successful natural philosopher on hypotheses as deduced from observations received considerable attention from practising scientists. Indeed, they persisted in some (distorted) form or another for the next two centuries.

A more critical examination of the practice of scientists reveals, however, overwhelming evidence to the contrary. It shows that science has no logic of discovery, no general procedure, nor simple continuous progress.[36] For instance, only Einstein produced the special and general theories of relativity, although the relevant knowledge was available to many of his contemporaries. In the case of the special theory, for example, he had to tap his own creativity in order to provide his several principles, to define his own operational procedures, and to advance conjointly along apparently divergent conceptual lines. Significantly, his achievements emphasized the role of the scientific principle or postulate. The same can be said of other great scientists, including Nicolaus Copernicus, Johannes Kepler, Galileo Galilei and Isaac Newton.

Nevertheless, the researches of the majority of scientists, at any given time, can probably be best described as basically unspectacular, essentially routine and logically consistent.[37] Deceptively, the unexpected result, the chance discovery, the thoughtless mistake, or the illogical leap sometimes integrates scientific thought. Any one of them can even catapult the scientist from relative obscurity to epochal eminence. Louis Pasteur's famous remark is always, of course, a realistic rider, "In this field of observation chance favours only the prepared mind."[38]

Having at last learned their lessons from science's history, many scientists recognise that science depends on the use of certain fundamental principles, which are educed neither from observations and experiments nor from logical and mathematical ratiocination. Most contemporary scientists also acknowledge that adherence to a single scientific method is a simplistic inhibitive misrepresentation. Scientific method is often described as if it were a set procedure. There is no such thing as *the* scientific method. This can be demonstrated by asking half a dozen eminently successful scientists who will outline six different methods. Something more than a standard prescription or a definitive description is needed to do justice to the modern scientific enterprise. In the twentieth century science is known to be a very complex endeavour.

Another common misconception among Christians is that scientists claim that scientific statements are necessarily certain. In this view, all scientific thinking is "not merely true or well-founded but indubitable."[1] Almost every natural scientist is familiar with the elementary aspects of non-Euclidean geometries, quantum theory and both the special and general theories of relativity. Probably he knows a little about Babylonian, Chinese, Egyptian, Grecian, Indian, Islamic and Sumerian contributions to the origin of modern science. He has learned, perhaps, a little more about the rise of modern science. Above all, he is acquainted with recent theoretical and experimental advances in his own specialism. Therefore, he recognises only too well the elusive nature of "certainty" in science, and will tend to avoid an ambiguous use of the word "truth"[39, 40]. In the words of Hermann Bondi, "My own inclination is that science has nothing to do with truth, but I am not sufficiently well versed in this to argue about it at any great length."[41] Of course, there are always gifted exceptions, like Albert Einstein, to any rule.

Modern scientists must come to terms with the ever-present Horation deficiency, the inability to acount for many important things in heaven and earth.[42] For instance, they must try to accommodate the rapidly increasing demands on the novice's ability to master enough existing science to reach the frontier. Otherwise their progeny may be unable to advance it. Somehow they must anticipate the possible physical or economic limitations which nature itself could impose on their capacity to secure data. Those engagements, and their like, leave little time to flirt with "certainty".

Nevertheless, a profound lesson learnable from every branch of science is that what "is inconceivable to one man, or in one age, is not necessarily so by another man, or in another period . . . Some discoveries which are unattainable in one age or state of knowledge become attainable in another; for instance, the laws of electro-magnetism or of electro-chemical action could not have been discovered when electro-currents were unknown, nor could the principle of the conservation of matter and of energy have been arrived at when science was in its infancy."[43] Science breaks new ground and improves the cultivation of old fields. That is its business. While certainty is elusive, hope is abundant.

According to Albert Einstein and Leopold Infeld, "nearly every great advance in science arises from a crisis in the old theory."[44] In the most significant cases "the new theory shows the merits as well as the limitations of the old theory and allows us to regain our old concepts from a higher level. This is true not only for the theories of electric fluids and fields, but for all changes in physical theories, however revolutionary they may seem . . . We can still apply the old theory, whenever the facts within its region of validity are investigated. But we may as well apply the new theory, since all the known facts are contained within the realm of its validity."[45] By directing attention to its realm of validity, Einstein could relate to both the demise of a scientific theory and its surviving applications without referring to "certainty" or recognising "revolutions".

Generally, scientists are motivated by the desire to apprehend, the need to believe and the will to search. "Throughout all our efforts, in every dramatic struggle between old and new views, we recognize the eternal longing for understanding, the ever-firm belief in the harmony of our world, continually strengthened by the increasing obstacles to comprehension."[46] Scientists thrive on "dramatic struggle" and know that "death alone can save one from making blunders."[47] New concepts, questions, problems, and theories are "born in the painful struggle with old ideas"[48] because "there are no eternal theories in science."[44]

Hence, hope, commitment and tenacity blossom in the absence of "certainty". Scientific thinking flourishes even as the scientific rank and file presently diminish. To demand "certainty" as a necessary condition of all scientific thinking is already to have misunderstood the nature of modern science. There is no need to claim longevity, let alone immortality, for any scientific theory. Its validity stands and falls as it points scientific investigation beyond itself toward greater precision and fuller apprehension.[49]

Through experience, both observational and experimental, scientists learn how to relate a particular datum to a definite cause. They believe that in doing so they are thinking scientifically. They are not philosophers, nor do they claim to be, although they are convinced that as scientists they behave rationally. As Einstein replied to the epistemologists, "(the scientist) accepts gratefully the epistemological analysis, but the external conditions which are set for him by the facts of experience, do not permit him to let himself be too much restricted in the construction of his conceptual world by adherence to an epistemological system."[50] For Einstein and a large number of practising scientists, scientific inferences are grounded in observational and experimental experiences. They are part of a freely created logical manifold.[51] They are *never indubitable*. *En masse* they represent what scientists believe is a relevant rational response to reality.[52]

Recognising, then, that a thought, statement or theory need not be certain to be scientific, it is appropriate to return to the problem of "truth" in science.[52] At the risk of offending some Christians by stating the seemingly obvious, it is a mistake to assume that scientific researchers identify the truth of a statement with its being scientific. Truth is *not sufficient* for scientific thinking.[52] As many post-graduate science students will confirm retrospectively, it is pointless to offer a conjecture to one's research superviser and expect that just because it happens to be true, he will accept it.

An anecdote from the physicist R. V. Jones illustrates the point neatly.[53] One night the research students of Francis Simon were working with liquid hydrogen in his laboratory. Shortly after midnight, there was an explosion causing extensive damage. One of the research students telephoned the professor to inform him of the accident. The only initial response he could get from Francis Simon was, "All right, I know what day it is!" It was the morning of April 1st. The frustrated research student was reminded that he must also provide adequate scientific grounds for the acceptance of a conjecture. Scientific statements are not conveniently labelled "true" or "false" for scientists.

Equally apparent, truth is *not necessary* for scientific thinking. As just noted, the assessment of a conjecture is a matter of examining its scientific grounds. For scientific researchers to claim that a statement or theory is scientific means that they are asserting that the basis on which it is to be accepted is the currently available scientific experience. When Isaac Newton's theory of gravitation was proposed, astronomers used it to predict the positions of planets and satellites and to forecast and retrodict eclipses. Originally published in 1687, "it was not until well into the eighteenth century that Newton's theory became generally accepted."[54] Gradually as the grounds for its acceptance were laid down – estimated by Bondi as well over a hundred thousand tests[55] – its scientific status grew. This occurred despite the considerable initial reservations about action at a distance, until by the middle of the nineteenth century it ruled supreme.

However, with the benefit of hindsight, specifically Einstein's theory of gravitation or one of its variants, it is now realised that while Newton's theory was scientific it was not the "truth". Even before the turn of the century evidence of its limitations was available to all who were familiar with the refined calculations of the advance of the longitude of the perihelion of Mercury's orbit.[56] Although consistent with a great wealth of empirical data, the demise of Newton's theory eventually came. It fell not simply as the "victim of the increasing precision of observation and calculation"[55] but as the glorious forerunner of a new and more powerful theory. Its defeasance is a salutary reminder to scientists that they should never again rest easy with the truth-content of any scientific theory.

There is, then, light at the end of the research tunnel. The birth of the general theory of relativity was dependent on the pre-existence of Newton's theory. Clearly, progress in scientific thinking cannot be adequately described as monotonically increasing with time, or as knowledge becoming more and more certain or true. But there is ample evidence to suggest that the scientists' reliance on the interaction of theory and experiment will continue. This interplay has long enabled them to move from existing theories describing ranges of phenomena to new theories encompassing even greater, but still limited, domains of experience.[55] Consequently, the vast majority of scientists are content to explore the intellectual uplands known as scientific thinking. The high peaks of "truth" and "certainty" they tend to leave for philosophers and theologians to tackle.

Nevertheless, there is a residual hankering. Born expressed it in the following way. "The scientist's urge to investigate, like the faith of the devout or the inspiration of the artist, is an expression of mankind's longing for something fixed, something at rest in the universal whirl: God, Beauty, Truth. Truth is what the scientist aims at. He finds nothing at rest, nothing enduring, in the universe. Not everything is knowable, still less predictable."[57] Perhaps the most impressive words of all came from Isaac Newton: " . . . I seem to have been only like a boy playing on the sea-shore, and diverting myself in now and then finding a smoother pebble or a prettier shell than ordinary, whilst the great ocean of truth lay all undiscovered before me."[58]

With the more obvious obstacles to a re-valuation of modern scientific thinking set aside, it is appropriate to sketch in broad strokes some of the many limitations of the present investigation.

5. ALBERT EINSTEIN, THE SKILLED GUIDE

Although very few scientists can, and less than a handful do, become an Albert Einstein, people of such calibre have commented on various aspects of scientific thinking, including the roles of "truth" and "certainty". Their deliberations bear a unique brand. They come from persons who are not restricted to talking *about* science. They are the reflections of individuals who have become eminently successful *in* science. Clearly, they have a special claim to relevance. Specifically, few scientists would challenge the view that Einstein was the most profound scientific thinker since the time of Newton. As an approach to modern scientific thinking, some of the published thoughts of Einstein are, therefore, presented together with selected comments from other distinguished scientists. In addition, granted that scientists should think scientifically, his explanation of why they should think scientifically is interpolated.

In his *Autobiographical Notes,* written in the evening of his remarkable life, Einstein gave his "credo" as his only concession to a systematic epistemology.[59] His "occasional utterances of epistemological content" are contained in numerous published articles, letters, and even quotations, making their integration difficult. Such an exercise probably runs counter to the better judgement of Einstein himself. However, if this attempt at thematic synthesis remains sensitive to Einstein's reservations, the interests of clarity and integrity will not be betrayed.

Some of the topics that are not addressed directly in this essay include the following: the role of the Michelson-Morley experiment in the origin of the special theory of relativity, the original contributions of Poincaré, Lorentz and Einstein to the special theory of relativity, Mach's influence on the conceptual development of Einstein, Einstein's understanding of the role of Mach's principle in the formulation of the general theory of relativity, Einstein's criticisms of quantum mechanics and his search for an unified field theory.

Those subjects would require such detailed investigations that they would inevitably carry the discussion too far afield. They would also court the danger of obscuring the unity, consistency and originality of Einstein's work, a hazard that is not without its victims. It is assumed that an acceptable evaluation of Einstein's views on scientific thinking will cast a feeble light on those matters. The present purpose is, however, to provide an answer to the preliminary question, "Why think scientifically?"

The inclusion of some comments from other scientists also merits a few words of explanation. In general, scientists do not claim to be philosophers or historians and philosophers of science. They draw almost exclusively on their scientific experience as they communicate their views on science and scientific thinking. Since this essay is an attempt to encourage Christians to read the extramural works of modern scientists, it makes references, where possible, to those equally acceptable sources rather than the more inaccessible academically respectable literature. Although they do not aspire to epistemological grandeur, the quotations selected show that working scientists have many instructive thoughts on the nature of science and scientific thinking. Therefore, they deserve a fair hearing from Christians. At the very minimum Christians can ask them to account for the intriguing observation that scientists of almost every conceivable philosophical persuasion have made significant advances in modern science.

To recap, most scientists are effectively laymen with respect to philosophies and histories of science. Very few have any claim even to the title of amateur theologian. Their scientific researches have probably been basically unspectacular, essentially routine and logically consistent. However, the contributions of Einstein raise for many of them several interesting questions. The answers are, of course, beyond the scope of this essay.

Why did the philosopher of science, Karl R. Popper acknowledge the importance of Einstein's scientific researches but, for the most part, ignore Einstein's available epistemological utterances? Did Popper, like the logical positivists, use Einstein's work and comments expediently? Did the scientist Michael Polanyi tacitly integrate his knowledge of Einstein's essays and researches? Or did Polanyi arrive later and independently at virtually identical bases for scientific realism? Is the historian of science Thomas S. Kuhn conceptually indebted to Einstein or Polanyi? Why are many modern introductions to epistemology and scientific realism silent about Einstein's writings, most of which were published well over forty years ago?

Of course, mere coincidence of views is no proof of influence, but the extent and context of a coincidence can imply some influence. More relevant in the present context is the obvious way in which those questions point to the importance of Einstein's contributions. While this essay merely hints at some possible answers to them they are placed starkly before the Christian customs officer to challenge at the outset his scales of valuation. Scientists are not philosophers, but they are quite definitely versatile rational thinkers. However, to learn from Einstein, this short essay does not end with blinding conclusions. Its unspecifiable but deliberate aim is to urge other Christians beyond its limitations and inadequacies to greater precision and fuller apprehension through the personal participation of interested parties.

6.   SCIENTISTS, THE UNCOMMUNICATIVE SOLITARY FELLOWS

To allay residual suspicion about the choice of Einstein as skilled guide rather than infallible authority, gross features of the personal dilemma of the academic researcher are silhouetted against the contradictory public image of the scientist as a dispassionate manipulator. By outlining Einstein's vocational kinship, awareness of his colossal scientific stature is heightened.

Earlier, reference was made to grand visions of a reciprocity between science and theology and a reconciliation of both with culture in general. On hearing these imaginative expressions of hope, many Christians will respond with a wry smile. To them such aspirations must sound rather like naive variations on an old theme. Apparently irreconcilable differences have long been signalled by the more conspicuous patterns of scientists' behaviour. Indeed, the social responsibility of scientists, or more precisely their supposed lack of it, has been a subject of controversy for centuries. Throughout that time, many scientific researchers have staunchly defended the view that scientific thinking requires freedom from humanitarian motivations. Consequently, in their professional capacities, they have tended to shy clear of direct societal involvements. Some of them have also claimed that scientists can exercise this freedom while denying all knowledge of it. It is hardly surprising to learn, therefore, that a large number of Christians have found and still find it difficult to relate to what appears to them as endemic social myopia.

According to many scientific researchers, society benefits and suffers as the consequences of scientific thinking are evaluated and utilized by applied "scientists" and technologists. In other words, they recognize legitimate but distinct roles for scientists and technologists. Somewhat enigmatically, if not arrogantly, most practising scientists believe that, in due course, the results of their researches will become vital to society, not by their direct intervention but through technological expertise.[60] Even "the most abstract and remote ideas may one day become of great practical importance – like Einstein's law of equivalence of mass and energy."[61] Still, the increasing number of difficulties is becoming progressively more acute as scientific achievements are ever more rapidly exploited by industry with ever less thorough assessments of the possible long-term and long-range effects. But they are neither the products nor the concerns of scientific research.[62]

The task of science is to describe, to the greatest possible extent, a reality in space-time which is independent of the perceiving subject.[63] However attractive and satisfactory scientific thinking appears, no matter how valuable scientific results may seem for the immediate material advantage of civilization, "it is most dangerous to apply these methods beyond the range of their validity, to religion, ethics, art, literature and all humanities . . ."[64] Scientific methods should be "restrict(ed) to that domain where they reasonably belong."

Scientific optimism should not be confused with the ill-informed popular optimism which regards the solutions to all humankind's problems as technological. The latter contrasts sharply with the much more realistic optimism of practising technologists and also with the more restricted optimism of scientists. Scientific optimism sees an increasing apprehension of the universe as an enrichment of life. It is based on what science has already accomplished through the labour and activity of scientists. It looks forward to a greater fulfilment which will entail the transformation of present scientific experience. Scientific optimism has its feet firmly on the ground of achievement and its head freely soaring in the air of anticipation.

Sheer hope propels scientific research. It also fosters the belief that scientific findings will eventually prove valuable to a modern highly mechanized civilization with its harnessable technological talents.[65] Yet, "hope is a word one hardly finds in the literature of (science). A paper starts with the planning of an experiment or with a theory based on expectation. But there is hardly any talk of hope." Born continued, "However, when I remember my actual experiences during a long scientific career, I have one inextinguishable memory: the disappointment when a result was different from what I had expected. But disappointment could only occur when there was hope."[66] Often, when discourse distrains, scientists fall back silently, perhaps complacently, on their optimism. Frequently they retire to the laboratory, the computer room or the library leaving the world to its own devices.

No doubt Christians are reasonably familiar with the apparently antisocial antics of scientists. Few of them volunteer for a debate for which they are neither properly prepared nor suitably equipped. They are trained for research, not dissemination. The former is objective, problematic, tangible and rewarding, while the latter promises to be subjective, argumentative, ambivalent and frustrating. Consequently, the vast silent majority of working scientists are content to leave the discussion of societal issues to a very small vocal competent minority of established figures.[67] Nevertheless, their task is not made any easier by disillusioned science graduates or disenchanted technologists excluded or released from scientific or industrial institutions. Further complicated by the speculative renderings of mass media career oriented popularizers, those circumstances are hardly optimal for progress towards a better mutual understanding among Christians and scientists.[68]

It is not easy to become one of the very small vocal competent minority of scientists who can present scientific subjects in an acceptable, authentic, popular manner. Einstein, who was an outstanding member of this fraternity, outlined "the great difficulties of such an attempt. Either (the scientist) succeeds in being intelligible by conceding the core of the problem and by offering to the reader (listener or viewer) only superficial aspects or vague allusions, thus deceiving the reader (listener or viewer) by arousing in him the deceptive illusion of comprehension or else he gives an expert account of the problem, but in such a fashion that the untrained reader (listener or viewer) is unable to follow the exposition and becomes discouraged from reading (listening or viewing) and further . . ."[69] The delicate art is to encourage a lively interest.

"It is of great importance that the general public be given an opportunity to experience – consciously and intelligently – the efforts and results of scientific research . . . Restricting the body of knowledge to a small group deadens the philosophical spirit of a people and leads to spiritual poverty."[69] Many scientists concede readily that there has been an abysmal failure on the part of scientists to communicate with the public at large. The situation will only degenerate further, however, if incompetent conflators and incomprehensible expositors are allowed to multiply indiscriminately. Consequently, scientists tend to err on the side of silence rather than risk joining the ranks of the misemployed.

Interested Christians could do more to encourage suitably gifted scientists to convey to non-scientists something of the joy, excitement and anticipation of scientific researches. Humankind stands miraculously between the macrocosm and the microcosm. *Homo sapiens* lives midway between the immensity of intergalactic space receiving its complex intimations from the distant past and the invisibility of atomic processes with their statistically predictable futures. Some scientists are more than capable of communicating their awareness of this experience as they run the rapids of scientific research. The need for them to do so surely cannot be overstated in an age when "spiritual poverty" takes the form of a moribund materialism. The whole world of difference between materialism and material well-being should be explained.

It is almost impossible to paint a realistic picture of the typical modern scientific researcher. Rigid generalisations about the scientist are misleading. They are insufficiently comprehensive and invariably arbitrary. What can be sketched about scientists does not offer much to encourage initiatives toward reconciliation. Generally it serves to reinforce low opinions of scientists' societal commitments. During an address delivered at a celebration of Max Planck's sixtieth birthday in 1918 before the Physical Society of Berlin, Albert Einstein spoke bluntly. "Most (scientists) are somewhat odd, uncommunicative, solitary fellows, really less like each other, in spite of common characteristics, than the hosts of the rejected."[70] With the future in their blood, their innubilous optimism sees little other than the eventual success and the ultimate importance of their researches.

Their tunnel-vision often taxes severely the patience and eyesight of colleagues, especially when their attempts to communicate depend on inadequately prepared slides.[71] On rare occasions, communication deteriorates drastically. The theoretician Eugene P. Wigner intimated that "(Wolfgang) Pauli was a brilliant lecturer if he prepared his address. Once when I invited him to address our colloquium in Princeton, he did not. The audience became restless and, feeling somewhat responsible for the event, I wanted to help out. He did not define the mathematical symbols he used and I thought that if he explained them, it would help us to understand what he was trying to present.

'Pauli,' I said, 'could you tell us again what your small a stands for?' (The 'again' was sheer politeness: he had not in fact defined it.)

Pauli was flabbergasted by my question and stood there speechless for a few seconds. However, he recovered. 'Wigner,' he said, 'you just have to know everything.'

The audience did not laugh."[72]

Of course, scientists manage, on the whole, to communicate their ideas. In this respect, they are a little like moles. Most of their time is spent in their own research tunnels. Consequently, on their brief, relatively infrequent excursions into the scientific limelight, they have to adapt to circumstances. Lack of time for adequate preparation, pre-occupation with current problems, eagerness to announce the most recent findings, the desire to convey both the breadth and intensity of a research project, and the demands and opportunities of the occasion are just some of the many variables to be taken into account. In this light, the infrequent misdemeanour is hardly surprising.

Since there is evidence of inattention to societal details within their ranks, even greater lapses are to be expected elsewhere. In an article dedicated to the astronomer F. M. Stratton on the occasion of his seventieth birthday, Born recorded a delightful anecdote about Karl Schwartzschild. A remarkably gifted astronomer and one of Born's teachers[73] Schwartzschild discovered the first "rigorous" solution to Einstein's field equations.[74] After informing his readers of the enthusiastic, versatile, all-embracing mind of Schwartzschild, Born began his tale.

A group of young professors and lecturers were in the habit of meeting for lunch at a certain table in a local restaurant not far from the Göttingen observatory. Until his marriage, Schwartzschild had been one of the group. Only a few weeks after the wedding, he was again in his favourite seat at the lunch table. Schwartzschild was deeply involved in a lively discussion about some scientific problem, when someone asked him: "Now, Schwartzschild, how do you like married life?" He blushed, jumped up, and said, "Married life – oh, I have quite forgotten – " then got his hat and ran away.[73] Many marriages are exposed to scientists' spasmodic lapses from domestic diligence. Familial sacrifices are not uncommon. Behind many scientists there are self-effacing partners and children who provide timeous encouragement and support.

Most scientists are deeply committed to and absorbed in their work.[75] Of course, scientists sometimes carry commitment too far. For instance, Born admitted at the International Relativity Conference in Berne in 1955: "I remember that on my honeymoon in 1913 I had in my luggage some reprints of Einstein's papers which absorbed my attention for hours, much to the annoyance of my bride. These papers seemed to me fascinating, but difficult and almost frightening."[76] Scientists tend to place a very high value on learning for its own sake, independent of any economic or social rewards.[77] Naturally, they have feelings like everyone else. They are sometimes appointed to a chair, elected a Fellow of the Royal Society, or awarded the Nobel Prize. Such mild discomforts are accommodated, but they are not the driving force to scientific research. The thrills of seeking and the joys of finding have to be experienced to be believed and safeguarded.

Science cannot flourish in a selfish, secretive climate. In fact, scientists are likely to find distasteful the competitiveness, expediency and personal restrictions of industry and governmental establishments.[77] They are liable to exhibit patterns of behaviour that they developed in childhood as reactions to personal isolation.[78] Probably adolescent lack of societal involvement influenced strongly their choice of a scientific vocation, precisely because it appealed to their already developing interest in things as opposed to people.[75]

A superb example of the intensity of scientists' interest in things was provided by the historian and philosopher of science, Herbert Dingle. " . . . A considerable earthquake occurred at Long Beach, not many miles from Pasadena, and the shock was distinctly felt there. I was in the office that had been allotted to me and at once hastened back to the Athenaeum to see if all was well. On the way I passed Einstein and Gutenberg a distinguished sesimologist who had come to work at Pasadena with the hope of experiencing an earthquake which he was unlikely to do in central Europe. They were standing on the campus closely examining a large sheet of paper. Only later did it transpire that what they had been studying was the plan of a sensitive new seismograph and they had been so absorbed in it they had failed to notice the earthquake!"[79]

The stubborn devotion of scientists to the pursuit of scientific "truth" is not a literary fiction. Unquestionably, it is better for a scientist to destroy privately his own illusions than to be publicly discredited by his colleagues. Besides, many scientists are naturally drawn to introspection and isolation.[80] Shades of those tendencies can be detected in Ernst Straus's account of an unusual exchange with Einstein. Straus reminisced: "(Einstein) had a firm conviction, which I do not think was justified, that he could explain (his ideas) to everybody. For instance, as I remember quite clearly, we were working on something in unified field theory and he came down rather cheerfully and said, 'I explained it this morning to my sister and she also thinks that it is a very good idea.' Now, his sister was a very intelligent woman, but she was a philologist and had not the slightest idea of any of his work. Since she was a very good listener, he liked to explain his newest ideas to her."[81] Most scientists must learn to cope with the frustration of being unable to articulate their deepest interests to those whom they love.

The ways in which scientists report their findings tend to hide rather than to reveal their personalities. They minimize personal unresolvable disputes, elevate logical aspects and repress emotions, opinions, preferences and intuitions.[82] The Nobel laureate, George Thomson admitted that, within the relative privacy of scientific circles, controversies in science have often been bitter and not always fairly conducted, but on the whole they have helped not hindered progress."[83] "Much of the misunderstanding of scientists and how they work is due to the standard format of articles in scientific journals. With the terse accounts of successful experiments and well-supported conclusions they show little of the untidy nature of research at the frontiers of knowledge."[84]

As scientists write up their researches for publication, they provide a scientific context by citing relevant published works. The latter are sometimes discerned in the light of new findings. An element of justification is involved, and possibilities for further studies are often indicated. Only pertinent details of the actual scientific discovery appear in the reported, standardized, repeatable methods as pale shadows of the original colourful course of events. Advisedly, scientific papers do not advocate such crudities as the precipitation of new compounds in the sink. The addition of a specified volume of freshly distilled water to a non-aqueous solution of known concentration at a definite temperature is much more scientific (and much less embarrassing for the discoverer). Of course, the checking of an experiment requires a knowledge of it. Consequently, there is logically speaking no such thing as rigorous repeatability.[85]

With the emphasis on objective reporting, scientific publications do not display the great gifts of persons like Isaac Newton, Michael Faraday or Ernest Rutherford. They "knew what to ask and how to pay attention not so much to what Nature was saying as to what Nature was whispering."[86] Nor do scientific papers or reviews capture such raptures as the rhapsodies of Ludwig Boltzmann on J. Clerk Maxwell, recorded in his contemplation of the latter's dynamical theory of gases.[87] In fact, "these are attitudes and feelings which every scientist knows are at the centre of scientific research."[84]

Scientists can only aspire to the economy of thought, the repeatability of action and the neutrality of scientific peer approval. As far as possible they avoid all unnecessary risks of lowering their productivity and reputation. Such consequences could result so easily from an uncharacteristic preoccupation with social action and comment. There is little sense in Churchmen or anyone else preaching to scientists on the role of social responsibility. Scientists have to deal primarily with objectivity, not ethics and morals.[88]

The morality of science is implied in its pursuit. The commitment of scientists to increased apprehensions of the non-moral universal order can only be expressed by the distinctive features of scientific thinking. They include thorough self-criticism and reliable reporting. Ethical questions about modern science are as difficult to ask as to answer. Too many unknowns cloud the issues. When scientists ask questions such as "What is the value of my work? What is the meaning of my vocation? What is the justification for my scientific research?", they can only give answers which rest ultimately on intuition and optimism. Attempts to do otherwise would demand too much diversification of effort beyond the bounds of scientific thinking. They would require, of course, the appropriate gifts, learning and, above all, motivation. Comparatively few scientists are so extensively equipped. The vast majority of scientists are convinced that the purpose of scientific research is to expand physical knowledge by first improving personal scientific understanding. It represents the desire to use to full advantage the human mind in apprehending nature.

It seems the bottom line reads that scientific performance and social involvement are inversely proportional for most scientists.[89] Scientific researchers, therefore, are extremely reluctant to change their characteristic spots. Holton put it succinctly when he wrote, "The major reason why some of these scientists can neglect the complex, tenuous long-range links that attach to their science is that they are so successful doing what they are doing. The short-range forces, which they master, completely saturate their capability for forming and perceiving long-range connections."[90]

Because so few scientists display an overt enthusiasm for "social responsibility" many Christians rashly conclude that all scientists are socially irresponsible. Some even believe that scientists are abetting the forces of cultural disintegration. Other than those who are experiencing the nightmare of statelessness, scientists are hard working citizens paying taxes. They are generally parents who are inevitably involved in concrete social responsibilities. By recognizing their limitations and concentrating on their specialisms, scientists avoid the abdication of their humanity. They express, through labour and activity, their beliefs that their particular disciplines have peculiarly important possibilities within the cultural matrix. They would probably recoil, however, from making their convictions explicit. Like Ulysses, the practising scientist binds himself to the mast of objective apprehension lest the siren song of "social responsibility" draws him overboard to drown in subjective speculation. In any case, too often in the past, the public statements of many accomplished scientists have met the united resistance of societal factions that had previously proclaimed diverse precognitions of "social responsibility".

It is in the natures of science, scientific thinking, and scientists themselves that they must remain somewhat detached from the immediacy of the interests, problems and concerns of humankind. Einstein often said that the ideal social position for an original thinker is to be a light-house keeper.[91] In equally picturesque Einsteinian terms, the "delicate little plant (of the curiosity of inquiry), aside from stimulation, stands mainly in need of freedom; without this it goes to wreck and ruin without fail. It is a very grave mistake to think that the enjoyment of seeing and searching can be promoted by means of coercion and a sense of duty."[92]

A rigorous analysis of the socio-political and economic framework of the scientific enterprise is beyond the wildest dreams of industrious scientific researchers. They know science as a human activity whose practice of discovery defies evaluation. Elitism, mysticism and egotism may intrude from time to time, but science has already outlived many generations of scientists and countless attempts at coercion.

To make contact with scientists, Christians should first try to understand a little of their work, thinking and vocational idiosyncrasies. In short, Christians should approach the scientist as a person with a vocation. "But the years of anxious searching in the dark, with their intense longing, their alterations of confidence and exhaustion and the final emergence into the light – only those who have experienced it can understand that."[93] Consequently, there is nowhere better to begin than with some of the thoughts, researches and characteristics of the world's most renowned twentieth century scientist.

Albert Einstein described frankly his perspective on the dilemma of the academic researcher as he honoured his old friend and colleague, Max Planck.

"A finely tempered nature longs to escape from personal life into the world of objective perception and thought; this desire may be compared with the townsman's irresistible longing to escape from his noisy, cramped surroundings into the silence of high mountains, where the eye ranges freely through the still, pure air and fondly traces out the restful contours apparently built for eternity.

"With this negative motive there goes a positive one. Man tries to make for himself in the fashion that suits him best a simplified and intelligible picture of the world; he then tries to some extent to substitute this cosmos of his for the world of experience, and thus to overcome it. This is what the painter, the poet, the speculative philosopher, and the natural scientist do, each in his own fashion. Each makes this cosmos and its construction the pivot of his emotional life, in order to find in this way the peace and security which he cannot find in the narrow whirlpool of personal experience."[70] Einstein's powerful insights are, so to speak, the fingerprints he left behind to show how he had carefully handled that fragile dilemma.

7. SCIENTIFIC CONCEPTS AS FREE CREATIONS

Much to the surprise, pleasure and enlightenment of lesser mortals, the brilliant physicist, Albert Einstein, found rather unusual ways of referring to his contact with reality. "All I have is the stubbornness of a mule; no, that's not quite all, I also have a nose."[94] Einstein's "nose" signified for him the ability to find and to follow the right track of scientific research. On the one side, his innate faculty for penetrating to the very heart of a problem and, on the other side, his native ability to recognise the significant implications of any hypothesis were probably sharpened to a keen edge by his work at the Swiss Patent Office. In Berne his duties demanded the patient rewording of applications and the definitive identification of their basic innovations.[95] It is small wonder that this intellectual giant came to believe so strongly that the task of a scientist is to find the most important question, and to pursue it without losing contact with the main problem.

Not only did he believe such things, he also practised them. His struggles for almost ten years in relative obscurity or effective isolation towards what became the special theory of relativity taught Einstein the value of "stubbornness". After a further seven years wrestling with the formative notions of the general theory of relativity he was even more attached to his "nose". Einstein had been seeking a unified field theory for the last seven years or more when, with great conviction, he told Hermann Weyl in 1923 that tracking was neither easy nor painless. "Mathematics are all well and good but nature keeps dragging us around by the nose."[96] With his unique brand of delightfully arresting humour carefully masking an acute sensitivity, Einstein made serious points about the deep problems of the role of experience in the origin of concepts and the function of concepts in ordering experience.

Concerned about the fundamental problem of "the eternal antithesis between the two inseparable components of knowledge, the empirical and the rational,"[97] Einstein reasoned that "the whole of science is nothing more than a refinement of everyday thinking."[98] He believed "that the first step in the setting of a 'real external world' is the formation of the concept of bodily objects and of bodily objects of various kinds. Out of the multitude of our sense experience we take, mentally and arbitrarily, certain repeatedly occurring complexes of sense impression . . ., and we attribute to them a meaning – the meaning of bodily object . . . logically this concept is not identical with the totality of the sense impressions referred to; but it is an arbitrary creation of the human . . . mind . . . the concept owes its meaning and its justification exclusively to the totality of sense impression that we associate with it."[99]

Einstein emphasized the creative aspect of thinking while indicating the necessarily personal interpretation of experience. Sense impressions are "given" as a "multitude" of prior indirect knowledge of reality requiring the creativity of the individual or scientist to bring order out of their lack of logical unity.[100] The creation of this order is also the process of explanation. According to Einstein, the best explanatory account of experience offers only highly warranted knowledge. Expressed differently, the creativity of the scientist produces a concept which integrates some range of the multitude of sense impressions to yield both limited meaning and justification.
justification.

Einstein explained "that one property which is characteristic of the notion 'bodily object' is the property which provides that we co-ordinate to it an existence, independent of (subjective) time, and independent of the fact that it is perceived by our senses. We do this in spite of the fact that we perceive temporal alterations in it."[101] Otherwise stated, when a real existence is attributed to a bodily object, it is given a significance which is largely independent of the sense impressions that originally gave rise to it. His creativity enables the scientist to decide what repeatedly occurring complexes of sense impressions are relevant to a given investigation. In current terms, facts are theory-laden[102], but, as far as Einstein was concerned, that was not the whole story. To risk obscuration, scientific apprehension "ultrasenses" and the senses of scientists "infrathink". Both kinds of activity span the logically unbridgeable gulf which separates the worlds of sensory experience and concepts. The empirical and rational contents of scientific knowledge are actually inseparable. With this belief, Einstein resolved the apparent tension between the logically free creation of a concept and the attribution to it of a real existence independent of the sense impressions that gave rise to it.

Conceptual systems are not just arbitrary sets of abstractions. They are empirically-loaded. Such an ascription is solely justified by the manner in which the concepts and the mental relations between them enable orientation in the labyrinth of sense impressions. It is never completely guaranteed, never absolutely certain.[99]

This implies that unproven beliefs lie at the basis of all knowledge. All characteristics of sense impressions are specified in relation to posterior constructions.[103] To say that a scientific statement is valid is to authorize its assertion which may or may not be legitimately made at a subsequent stage in conceptual development. In other words, the concepts that arise in scientific thinking, statements and theories are logically free creations of the human mind, free inventions of the human intellect, that cannot be derived inductively from sensory experience.[104] On the other hand, purely logical thinking cannot by an operation within its province provide knowledge of the world of experience. All knowledge of reality begins and terminates in experience.[104] Einstein challenged the traditional prejudice that the mind trained in logic and language can achieve meaningful results in all fields of human endeavour without recourse to experience. He rejected *a priori* approaches to scientific knowledge as attacks on its empirical contents.

Scientific concepts both order and survey experience. They are tested by their success in structuring the manifold of sense experiences. Scientific knowledge is neither accessible through pure thought alone nor can it be gained through the senses alone. Einstein rejected the notion of purely inductive reasoning. He also dismissed the ideas of hypotheses readily verifiable or falsifiable by immediate experience. Instead, he concentrated on the intrinsically constructive and inherently co-ordinative elements of rational conceptualization. His concern was for the scope and creativity of scientific thinking. Both are ultimately dependent on the personal apprehension of the scientist. The detailed psychological aspects of his experiences are, for scientific intents and purposes, largely eliminated.[105] However, the constructive nature of concepts leaves them open to the danger of being obscured by the everyday habits of combining certain concepts and conceptual relations definitely with specific sensory experiences.[106]

In what Einstein jokingly referred to as his own obituary, his autobiographical essay in *Albert Einstein: Philosopher-Scientist* (editor: P. A. Schlipp), he actually raised the question, "What, precisely, is thinking?".[107] For him neither the emergence of memory pictures at the reception of sense impressions, nor a series of such pictures – each member calling forth another – has crossed the threshold of thinking. They furnish the raw material from which concepts are constructed. The appearance of a particular picture in many such series becomes an ordering element for such a series by connecting the otherwise unconnected series. "Such an element becomes an instrument, a concept."[107]

Einstein's reference to a concept as an instrument has profound implications. It likens the free conceptual play of the natural scientist to the skilful activity of the painter, the poet and the speculative philosopher, comparisons that he made explicitly elsewhere.[70] Einstein was sensitive to both the presence of hidden qualities in the scientist and the existence of undiscovered order in nature. Somehow the combination of those two guided scientists in their researches.

The particulars of a skill are generally unspecifiable, although the person is never ignorant of them. With such comparisons in mind, Einstein suggested that his own associative conceptual play involved elements "of visual and some of muscular type."[108] Full consciousness of such activity appeared to him to be "a limit case which can never be fully accomplished," because of what he termed the "narrowness of consciousness".[108] "Especially, in research thought, do mental pictures or internal words present themselves in the full consciousness or in the fringe-consciousness . . .?"[108]

Scientists organize their conceptual reactions to the natural order in ways similar to the co-ordination of muscular and visual responses during skilful activity. The highly pertinent common characteristics of all types of process is the presence of non-articulate conceptual elements. These elements are responsible for the fluidity of concepts and theories. Inveterate habits and routine responses always introduce rigidity at the expense of heuristic attentiveness. If a system of concepts, or a theory, is regarded as a closed immutable entity, then the definable, operational characteristics of its concepts have effectively eclipsed its cosmic connections. The resulting "certainty" is unreal and frustrates further striving.

According to Einstein, scientific theories have something in common with the images of the poet. Both stimulate the intuition of the individual as resources for the apprehension of reality. Basically, any scientific theory embodies aspects of reality that are not explainable in terms of that theory. Scientific theories are not comprehensive instruction manuals. They survey empirical knowledge but necessarily with limited logic and precision. Scientific research is always returning from abroad with intimations of new continents, their differing phenomena, and the novelty of their diverse life-forms. Scientists glimpse aspects of the natural order through the limited logical unity of scientific theories which always point beyond themselves. In short, Einstein's notion of a concept presupposes the rationality of the universe, without which it would have no vital future. On this presupposition rests the fundamental faith from which all scientific hope springs. Like artists who envisage their creations by working confidently toward them, scientists create their visions of the hidden pattern of the physical world and labour optimistically to refine their concepts of that reality.

The transition from free association of sense impressions, memory pictures, or images to thinking is characterized by the essentially dominating role of concept. But, as indicated, a concept need not be correlated with "a sensorily cognizable and reproducible sign (word)," although it is through such correlations that thinking becomes communicable.[107] Private thought does not necessarily wait for this stage. On the contrary, it "goes on for the most part without the use of signs (words) and beyond that to a considerable degree unconsciously."[107] Each particular concept seems to be originally a heuristic probe or a cognitive compass, but not a map. It assists, so to speak, navigation through the uncharted inexpressible deep of private thought.

Conscious of muscular and visual analogies, Einstein always maintained that the pre-articulate phase of conceptualization was not amenable to exact formulation. Under those circumstances scientists engage in the heuristics of apprehension while denied what have yet to become the definable, operational characteristics of conceptualization. They breathe, as it were, the scientific atmosphere while exploring its chemistry. Even as they enmesh new instruments or concepts as a logical complex of concepts, their non-verbal and intrinsically heuristic aspects are retained. Those aspects of conceptual innovations remain partially unrealised by virtue of their elusive empirical connectivity. Just as a description of a person cannot acquaint one with him, so a definition of a scientific concept cannot provide an exhaustive understanding of it. Scientists must live alongside it to learn how it behaves in a variety of circumstances. Scientific concepts are never comprehensively exposable to lucid critical inspection because of the nature of their contacts with reality. Their empirical grounding ensures that scientific concepts are fundamentally non-arbitrary, although from a logical point of view, they are free creations of the human mind. Consequently, concepts must be discovered. They cannot be made. Throughout Einstein's writings, he talks consistently of the discovery of scientific concepts and theories. By personal participation scientists grasp the bearing of concepts on experience and expand their visions of the "eternally unattainable in the field of scientific endeavours."[109]

Conventional words or other signs are involved, according to Einstein, at a secondary stage after the concepts are secured and reproducible.[108] Only when a concept has been caught in a logical net does it become definable, quantitative and operational. As already noted, it retains its heuristic character by virtue of its qualitative connectivity.[110] Defined concepts have, therefore, a heuristic coefficient of meaning. In fact, their continued survival ultimately depends on their connectivity to undefined aspects of other complexes of concepts. This openness means that the scientist need not be trapped in the "narrow whirlpool of personal experience."[70] Indeed, his apprehension of the natural order represents a constitutive characteristic of knowledge. Progressively the scientist detaches himself from self-centred passions and illusions by the very practical pursuit of objective knowledge of the universe. In doing so, he nurtures his "sympathy with the natural order."[111] Ultimately, scientists rely, not on themselves, but on reality. By striving to submit to an independent reality through the co-ordinative role of concepts, scientific thinking rises above the "merely personal"[112] to the level of the personal, above the subjective to the rational. Subjectivity is avoided by the universal reference of the scientist's participation.

8. SCIENTIFIC THEORIES OR GAMES

As far as Einstein was concerned, "all our thinking is of the nature of free play with concepts; the justification for this play lies in the measure of survey over the experience of the senses which we are able to achieve with its aid. The concept of 'truth' cannot yet be applied to such a structure; to my thinking this concept can come in question only when a far-reaching agreement (convention) concerning the elements and rules of the game is already at hand."[113] Einstein was pointing through the visible, audible manipulations of thought to its grounding in reality. His repeated use of the word "play" keeps to the fore the notion that the meaning of scientific research lies in itself. Scientists don't work at conceptualization. They delight in playing at it. In other words, their awareness is primarily of reality not just of some particular task. According to Einstein, scientists are struck by thoughts as well as observations. In scientific thinking, Einstein found not only a logical manifold but also a heuristic dynamics.[51] A heuristic play requires the refinement of apprehension by expanding the logical survey through a responsive re-ordering or re-interpretation of experience. It is intrinsically irreversible because the scientist experiences a growing sympathy with the natural order.

To use an analogy, the scientist travels along a continuous series of conceptual hysteresis loops as his theories are variously created during every cycle. In principle, each loop begins with a heuristic departure from an established theory. The vehicle is an original non-articulate concept. This venture is a creative act of faith. A formalizing return carries apprehension beyond the old theory to its successor. This activity produces an expanded logical survey. Both halves of the cycle must be traversed before a new theory is discovered. In reality, it is difficult to isolate the two movements. Without the continual heuristic tremor action of the mind's eye, creativity disappears. The discovery of a scientific theory exercises both creativity and analysis. It also stimulates the expectation and intuition which lead to experimentation and the next cycle.

In plain terms, how does one actually arrive at what Einstein called the rules of a scientific game? As indicated, Einstein's discussion of scientific thinking starts with the memory picture and the concept of bodily object of everyday thinking. The refinement of thinking, he believed, was achieved by means of levels or strata of knowledge. On the fundamental level, common to everyday thinking and the first phase of scientific development, concepts are directly connected with sense experience and their inter-relating theorems.[114] The concepts and theorems of all strata are "from the point of view of logic freely chosen conventions . . . The relations between the concepts and propositions among themselves and each other are of a logical nature, and the business of logical thinking is strictly limited to the achievement of the connection between concepts and propositions among each other according to firmly laid down rules which are the concern of logic."[115]

"While the rules themselves are arbitrary, it is their rigidity alone which makes the (scientific) game possible. However, the fixation (of the rules) will never be final. It will have validity only for a special field of application."[114] There are, in principle, an unlimited number of games involving different rules, concepts and their relations. None of them can be regarded as providing absolutely certain knowledge. Judgements of significance and coherence can be made only within a scientific game. A scientific game is heuristically active when it prompts scientific players in other games to alter their rules to improve those conceptual systems. Nevertheless, those players only change the rules as they pursue the rationality of the universe in which all scientific games are rooted. In any particular game, the concepts that are directly and intuitively connected with complexes of sense experiences are called primary concepts. All other notions are connected with them by theorems and derive their meaning by virtue of these connections. They are "statements about reality" in so far as they express "indirect relations beween primary concepts, and in this way between sense experiences."[115]

Einstein provided an illustration of the two indispensable characteristics of scientific theories. "Suppose an archaeologist belonging to a later culture finds a textbook of Euclidean geometry without diagrams. He will discover how the words 'point,' 'straight-line,' 'plane,' are used in propositions. He will also recognise how the latter are deduced from each other. He will even be able to frame new propositions according to the rules he recognised. But the framing of these propositions will remain empty play with words for him so long as 'point,' 'straight-line,' 'plane,' etc., convey nothing to him. Only when they convey something will geometry possess any real content for him . . ."[116]

" . . . This extra-logical problem is the problem of the nature of geometry, which the archaeologist will only be able to solve intuitively by examining his experience for anything he can discover which corresponds to those primary terms of the theory and the axioms laid down for them. Only in this sense can the question of the nature of a conceptually presented entity be reasonably raised."[116] Logical investigation cannot reveal the connections between theories and experience. It can only show how concepts relate to one another. Their empirical contacts endow theories with real content. Clearly, Einstein looked beyond algorithms to empirical grounds for the truth-contents of scientific theories.

According to Einstein, the search for greater logical unity in the world picture characterizes scientific thinking. It cannot rest content with the established standards of everyday thinking.[100] Aiming at as complete an apprehension of the totality of sense experiences as possible, science strives for "the use of a minimum of primary concepts and relations."[100] Scientists invent systems progressively poorer in concepts and relations, but retaining the primary concepts and their relations as logically derived concepts and relations. They arrive at systems of considerably greater logical unity. The latter are still compatible with complexes of sense experiences. In such an enterprise, heuristically poorer intermediate levels gradually disappear with a concomitant loss in ease of understanding. As Einstein explained in a letter to a student of philosophy, "it is true that the grasping of truth is not possible without empirical basis. However, the deeper we penetrate and the more extensive and embracing our theories become the less empirical knowledge is needed to determine those theories."[117] Each new theory surrenders previously accessible modes of apprehension, introduces more intricate mathematical methods and postulates the existence of new processes not necessarily open to immediate scientific investigation.[118]

An outstanding case in point is the sequence of transitions from Newton's laws of motion to the special theory of relativity and to the general theory of relativity. In Einstein's words, "The theory of relativity is a fine example of the fundamental character of the modern development of theoretical science. The initial hypotheses become steadily more abstract and remote from experience. On the other hand, it gets nearer to the grand aim of all science, which is to cover the greatest possible number of empirical facts by logical deduction from the smallest possible number of hypotheses or axioms. Meanwhile, the train of thought leading from the axioms to the empirical facts or verifiable consequences gets steadily longer and more subtle. The theoretical scientist is compelled in an increasing degree to be guided by purely mathematical, formal considerations in his search for a theory, because the physical experience of the experimenter cannot lead him up to the regions of highest abstraction."[119] Einstein recognized that the further scientific theories are removed from the empirical data the more they are underdetermined by the narrow selections of those data. This trend increases the scientist's dependence on mathematical and formal criteria. The latter, of course, represent highly sophisticated contacts with empirical data. The development of modern science does not follow, however, a simple hierarchical pattern of conceptual complexity.

9. JOHANNES KEPLER: A PARTICULARLY FINE EXAMPLE

To summarize the two preceding sections and to illustrate their direct bearing on scientific research, Einstein's two articles on Johannes Kepler are correlated. Einstein underscored the greatness of Kepler's achievement by outlining "his problem and the stages of its solution."[120] As he did so, Einstein demonstrated both the dominant role of concept in Kepler's work, and its dependence on "purely mathematical, formal considerations."[119] This exercise also shows the consistency and coherence of Einstein's thought over a considerable period of time.

Kepler spent "decades of hard and patient work"[120] wrestling with the problem of "the empirical investigation of planetary motion and the mathematical laws of that motion."[120] In other words, he struggled with a particular manifestation of the fundamental problem of "the eternal antithesis between the two inseparable components of knowledge, the empirical and the rational."[97] "Out of the multitude" of the observations and records compiled with such care by Tycho Brahe, Kepler has to bring "order" and explanation.[121] Actually, these data "dealt not with the movements of the planets in space but with the temporal shifts undergone by the direction earth-planet in the course of time."[122] But Kepler held an unproven belief in the heuristic power of the Copernican system with the sun regarded as at rest and the planets, including the earth, revolving about it. Indeed, his heliocentric perspective raised the problem of the determination of the motions of the planets as they might appear to an observer on the nearest fixed star.[122] As Einstein pointed out, this problem had to be solved before Kepler could begin to formulate the mathematical laws governing the planetary motions.[122]

Kepler constructed as "an arbitrary creation of the human mind"[121] the concept of "the straight sun-earth line."[123] He used it as an "element" or "instrument."[107] Kepler ascertained how its direction changed in the course of the year. He discovered that these directions lay in "a plane stationary with reference to the fixed stars and that the angular velocity of the sun-earth line varied in a regular way . . ."[123] The achieved "measure of survey"[107] over the observations both justified the construction of, and gave meaning to, the concept of "straight sun-earth line."

Kepler also realized "from observations of the sun that the

apparent path of the sun against the fixed stars differed in speed at different times of the year, but that the angular velocity of this movement was always the same at the same time of the astronomical year, and, therefore, that the speed of rotation of the straight line earth–sun was always the same when it pointed to the same region of the fixed stars."[123] He associated with these "repeatedly occurring"[121] conditions the concept of a closed planetary orbit. This heuristic device, "which was by no means obvious *a priori*"[124], imposed a restriction. At the end of each planetary year the planet returned to the same position in planetary space. With the available data on Mars Kepler was able to use this fixed point and that of the sun as reference points for the calculation of angular magnitudes.[125] By employing the standard methods of triangulation and assuming that space was Euclidean, he "discovered the true shape of the earth's orbit and the way in which the earth described it."[126] Identical procedures were applicable to the other planets. In this phase of his work, Kepler "determined empirically"[126] the planetary orbits.

To establish "from the empirical data"[126] the laws of planetary motions, he had to select a mathematical curve to describe the orbit. He tested his selection against the data, and repeated the process until an acceptable solution was found. In other words, "Kepler had first to recognize that even the most lucidly mathematical theory was of itself no guarantee of truth, becoming meaningless unless it was checked against the most exacting observations in natural science."[127] Although ultimately dependent on his personal apprehension of the universe, Kepler realized that the scope and creativity of his scientific thinking had to be grounded in the observed data. "After tremendous search, the conjecture that the orbit was an ellipse with the sun at one of its foci was found to fit the facts. Kepler also discovered the law governing the variation in speed during one revolution, which is that the line sun–planet sweeps out equal areas in equal periods of time. Finally he discovered that the squares of the periods of revolution round the sun vary as cubes of the major axes of the ellipses."[126] While skilfully exercising his hidden qualities as a scientist, Kepler detected the existence of previously undiscovered order in nature by looking through and beyond the Copernican system.

"Kepler lived in an age in which the reign of law in nature was as yet by no means certain."[120] He freed himself from traditional habits of mind with "his faith in the existence of natural law."[120]

This faith combined with a heliocentric perspective derived from Copernicus[120] to sustain and to guide him in his "search for a greater logical unity in the world picture."[100] His Copernican vantage point was, so to speak, "abstract and remote from experience."[119] Kepler was compelled, therefore, "to be guided by purely mathematical considerations in his search for a theory, because the physical experience of the experimenter cannot lead him up to the regions of highest abstraction."[119] In general terms, "the mysterious harmony of nature into which we are born"[126] enables "the human mind to construct forms independently before we can find them in things. Kepler's marvellous achievement is a particularly fine example of the truth that knowledge cannot spring from experience alone but only from the comparison of the inventions of the intellect with observed fact."[128] Obviously, "the mysterious harmony into which we are born" played a fundamental role in Einsteinian thought. Indeed, it merits considerable attention.

10. THE INTUITIVE RELATION

Belief in an external world independent of the observer is, in Einstein's opinion, the foundation of all science.[128] This assertion takes precedence over all others. The objectivity of scientific research is the on-going discovery of the rationality of the universe. It is subordinate to the given natural order which always transcends current scientific apprehension. The development of science had demonstrated to Einstein's satisfaction that among all conceivable constructions at a given time, one had proved itself to be unconditionally superior. This is Einstein's exclusion principle which depends on much more than observational and experimental evidence.

Science "can teach us nothing beyond how facts are related to, and conditioned by, each other. The aspiration toward such objective knowledge belongs to the highest of which man is capable . . . Objective knowledge provides us with the powerful instruments for the achievements of certain ends, but the ultimate goal itself and the longing to reach it must come from another source."[129] Einstein was fully convinced that commitment to the scientific enterprise has roots that run much deeper than current objective scientific knowledge. This commitment is perficient and pre-reflective. Although no logical path leads from perceptions to theory, the world of perceptions practically determines the theoretical system.

It does so through intuition which feeds a growing sympathy with the natural order.[111] Scientific researchers combine penetrating intuition and personal assessment, as they respond to an irrepressible commitment to make greater contact with reality.

Meeting with Einstein's approval, Victor Lenzen re-affirmed that "the relational structure of an independent reality can be cognised by virtue of a pre-established harmony between thought and reality."[130] Einstein's conceptual debts to both his former professor Hermann Minkowski[131] and the founder of quantum theory Max Planck[132] are obvious. This pervasive harmony imposes an important restriction. For a physical theory to be complete, every element of physical reality must have a counterpart in the physical theory. In this view, modern science appears as, at most, the pursuit of truth. The attainment of truth would require the comprehension of reality. But scientists are always immersed in more sense experiences than they can cope with at any given moment. They must repeatedly decide, therefore, to disregard some of them and to pre-select others. How they do so depends on the particular stage of scientific development.

The grasping of what is significant in physical theories is not exclusively governed by the condition that "the theory must not contradict empirical facts."[133] There is an obvious but entirely arbitrary and unsatisfactory way of meeting this demand. The rejection of a general theory can be deferred indefinitely by resorting to the use of "artificial additional assumptions."[133] Those artifices adapt the established theory to new empirical data. With such options almost invariably open, this particular criterion is seldom, if ever, sufficient for the confirmation or refutation of a theory. In any case it is limited by its dependence on available empirical data. The latter are themselves pre-selected through theory-laden observations and experiments. In fact, as Holton has consistently explained for nearly twenty years, Einstein had definite scientific occasion to draw attention to those very weaknesses.[134]

In defense of the special theory of relativity, Einstein maintained[135] that the incompatible experimental results of Walter Kaufmann[136] were insufficient in scope and diversity to warrant a final verdict. He argued that, although those results did match more closely the predictions of the rival theories of electron motion of A. H. Bucherer and Max Abraham, these theories were not integral parts of a much more extensive theoretical system. As things turned out, Kaufmann's equipment was inadequate and Einstein's theory became generally accepted. What is highly pertinent to the present discussion is that Einstein placed a far greater emphasis on factors other than any correspondence of theory with "empirical facts." In plain language, Einstein rejected the experimental results of Kaufmann in favour of the formal merits of his own theory. Einstein believed that scientific wisdom includes and supervenes upon the apprehension of scientific fact. He denied that scientific thinking is exclusively analytical. By implication, he dissociated himself from all philosophies and histories of science which insist on the refutability of scientific theories by experimental evidence alone.

Three quarters of a century ago, Einstein argued effectively in the scientific literature that scientific theories cannot be justifiably abandoned solely because a series of counter-instances is discovered.[137] Yet according to Karl R. Popper writing decades later, the characteristic feature of science is its bifurcated process of discovery.[138] This process is supposedly sharply divided into the inexplicable non-rational choice of a hypothesis, conjecture, or guess[139] and the strict testing of the chosen conjecture. By deducing consequences from such an hypothesis deliberate attempts can be made to refute it. In this view, refutation is logically possible, while confirmation is not.[140] Popper believes that competent scientists are continually submitting their conjectures to criticism. Apparently they are invariably prepared to drop their guesses like hot potatoes as soon as they are refuted. According to Popper, the testing of scientific theories serves the growth of knowledge by leading to sounder and maturer theories of increasing content but decreasing probability.[141]

Popper and Einstein agreed that scientific thinking does not require truth and certainty. They disagreed markedly, however, on what counts as telling contrary scientific evidence. Popper, the philospher of science, concentrates on the logical aspects of published scientific studies. For him, a counter-instance is sufficient to falsify an universal hypothesis. Einstein, the practising scientific researcher, valued the intuitive relation. According to him, there were other equally significant scientific matters to be considered beyond the strict testing of scientific theories. Einstein believed in a mediated type of knowledge which informed an appetitive sensibility to non-quantitative intimations of reality. In fact, the dispassionate negativism of Popper contrasts sharply with the committed optimism of Einstein. The former irrationalized scientific discovery, while the latter relished its prospects.

In his defense of the special theory of relativity Einstein appealed to a second criterion, "not concerned with the relation to the material of observation but with the premises of the theory itself."[133] Defying "exact formulation," this criterion relates to what Einstein referred to as the "naturalness" or "logical simplicity" of the "basic concepts and of the relations between these which are taken as a basis."[133] It concerns the "inner perfection" of the theory, whereas the first criterion refers to the "external confirmation" of the theory. Einstein differentiated clearly between the criticisms of a theory and the grounds offered for it. For example, he realized that in his special (and general) theory of relativity causal relationships are determinate, but that causality is unobservable. The intuitive relation which expresses his unshakable belief in the knowability of the universe ensures that causality as a logically free creation, need not be observable in order to be meaningful. With this distinction the profound significance of the pre-established harmony between thought and reality begins to emerge.

The bold intuitions of scientists involve private associations, preferences and even preconceptions. They are free creations of the human mind but only within this greater given order. The pervasive structure of that order presents through the intuitive relation all that scientists seek to apprehend. As already noted, it is always greater than what they can define and quantify. When scientists explore the unknown and encounter the unexpected, they are guided "to a considerable degree unconsciously" by its comprehensive rationality. In this view, scientists participate personally in the act of assimilating knowledge. The intuitive relation implies that scientific knowledge cannot be wholly explicit. It is never "objective" in the sense that its content is entirely determined by observation and experiment. A scientist's intuitive grasp of the significance of a theory depends on "a kind of weighing of incommensurable qualities."[133] It involves assaying the various relevant factors and reaching a rational decision where certainty is not possible.[142]

Clearly, scientific thinking is not impersonal, abstract, and disembodied. It requires much wider cognitive powers than traditional conceptions of knowledge would suggest. It is, of course, the relation of the intuitive and explicit components of scientific knowledge that allows for the existence of unspecifiable notions like "naturalness" or "inner perfection." This unspecifiability is the characteristic of scientific thinking with which Einstein grappled. It has been largely ignored or severely underrated by many who have subsequently offered descriptions of modern scientific methods. Theoretical statements are never equivalent to sets of observation statements. In fact, the former relate to reality in an indefinite variety of ways. Observational predictions are not rigorously warranted by a theory. Indeed, as already implied, Einstein rejected the naive view that the success of a scientific theory can be judged exclusively on the basis of prediction and control. Unknown factors are always operative during any scientific investigation. This precludes pre-established rules to determine the fate of a theory or hypothesis in the event of experimental failure. Still the scientific enterprise is in very good health.

Convinced of the reality of an independent universal order, whose rationality they can only partially intuit at any given moment, scientists often judge a theory on the basis of non-quantitative tokens of reality. The latter include conceptual beauty, correlative capacity and heuristic connectivity. Scientists relate to the economic, systematic and intimative qualities of a theory, particularly in the absence of immediate extensive empirical contact. "A theory is the more impressive the greater the simplicity of its premises, the more different kinds of things it relates, and the more extended is its area of applicability."[143] It was precisely on those grounds that Einstein planted the flag for the special theory of relativity. He did not regard scientists as the modern intellectual equivalents of primitive big-game hunters. According to Einstein, scientists do not run their conceptual quarry, the scientific theory, to a stand-still in the heat of the empirical day in order to kill it and discard its exposed framework. Nor did he offer a simple account of science as based on an unshakable foundation of fact. On the contrary, he stressed repeatedly that scientists cannot construct with certainty the accumulating laws of nature by means of a well defined logic or a tailor-made method. Only in recent decades have philosophers of science been sensitized to the tentative and transformative aspects of twentieth century science, characteristics to which Einstein responded with the intuitive relation so long ago.

The pre-established harmony between thought and reality is effectual through personal intuition. It is operative not just in the mature criticism of physical theories but throughout the working lives of scientists. Its impact is felt in the very early stages of their intellectual development. In fact, Einstein believed that we are born into the mysterious harmony of nature.[126] He drew attention to his own remarkable intuitive ability in physics "to differentiate clearly the fundamentally important, that which is really basic," from "the multitude of things which clutter the mind and divert the essential."[144] His apparent lack of it in mathematics strongly influenced his decision to become a physicist.[144] According to Einstein, the possibility of seeing a problem or focusing the most significant aspects of a subject depended on his intuitive ability to frame proper questions and to make legitimate associations. Both searching questions and innovative associations helped him to span the logical gap.

As a student of physics, he was much more impressed by "the achievements of classical mechanics in areas which apparently had nothing to do with mechanics" than by "the technical construction of classical mechanics or the solution of complicated problems."[145] Einstein did not isolate the tackling of a particular problem, or the study of a specific topic, from the general scientific context. His greater visions provided him, even as an apprentice, with vital wider intimations of universal order. The validity of a scientific statement, solution or theory depends on more than its local legitimation. It relies also on its broader capacity to reveal reality or to guide an intuited sense of hidden implications. According to Einstein, scientists cannot meaningfully study valid theories without at least considering their bearing on the immediate corpus of scientific knowledge.

In an article entitled *"On the Generalized Theory of Gravitation,"* Einstein raised the following questions. "What, then, impels us to devise theory after theory? Why do we devise theories at all?"[148] He offered the following answer. "New theories are first of all necessary when we encounter new facts which cannot be 'explained' by existing theories. But this motivation for setting up new theories is, so to speak, trivial, imposed from without. There is another, more subtle motive of no less importance. This is striving towards unification and simplification of the premisses of the theory as a whole (i.e. Mach's principle of economy, interpreted as a logical principle)."[148]

A passion for apprehension motivates scientists. In comparison with the intuitive searching of scientists, the discovery of new facts plays a relatively minor role in the construction of scientific theories. Einstein was convinced, for instance, that without the principle of general relativity no amount of collections of facts could lead to the equations of general relativity.[149]

As an accomplished researcher, Einstein reminisced that he had

had "no serious doubts" about the strict validity of "the law of the equality of inertial and gravitational mass" even "without knowing the results of the admirable experiments of Eötvös, which – if my memory is right – I only came to know later."[146] "Never one to give excessive weight to observations"[147], Einstein placed all his scientific hope in "the discovery that a reasonable theory of gravitation" could only be obtained "from an extension of the principle of relativity."[147] Once again Einstein assumed the fundamental point that concepts are discovered, not made. Obviously the discovery of the concept of an extension of the principle of relativity was initially unspecifiable. It developed from Einstein's interpretation of the significance of the equality of inertial and gravitational mass. In other words, he committed himself to a non-arbitrary, non-verifiable, non-falsifiable hypothesis. His strategy successfully led him to the general theory of relativity. The insatiable desire to understand more fully the rationality of the universe by ordering more consistently the ever-changing facts, observations, and experiments is the motivation behind all science. The intensity of the scientist's "sympathetic understanding" of the natural order reflects his passion for apprehension.

Einstein indicated a little of the nature of the role of the pre-established harmony between thought and reality. But he made no attempt to explicate its detailed functions. On the contrary, he was "satisfied with the mystery of the eternity of life and with the awareness and a glimpse of the marvellous structure of the existing world, together with the devoted striving to comprehend a portion, be it ever so tiny, of the Reason that manifests itself in nature."[150] In fact, he believed that it was not possible to say anything about the exact way in which concepts are formed and connected or about how they are coordinated to experiences.[151] Einstein was convinced that important, unspecifiable elements are at work in scientific knowledge. Einstein was content, therefore, to fall back on explicit qualitative consequences of the intuitive relation. The existence of the higher harmony between thought and reality could not be proved. Nevertheless, he was prepared to make extraordinary scientific hypotheses, non-arbitrary, non-falsifiable, non-verifiable commitments based ultimately on his prior scientific preferences.[152] Einstein did so particularly in what could be described as scientific emergencies when only a transfusion of intuition could save the corpus of scientific knowledge.

Einstein was not unique in this respect. For example, his old friend and fellow physicist, Born admitted freely, "My attitude to statistics in quantum mechanics is hardly affected by formal logic, and I venture to say that the same holds for Einstein. That his opinion in this matter differs from mine is regrettable, but it is no object of logical dispute between us. It is based on different experience in our work and life."[153] However, if Einstein's good news is that the intuitive relation is operative throughout the working lives of scientific researchers, his bad news is that scientific researchers are unavoidably exposed to delusion and fantasy.

11. DELUSIONS AND FANTASIES

From an Einsteinian perspective, there is always a tension between the logical and creative elements of scientific thinking. The connection between concepts and sense impressions is not of a logical nature. It should not be obscured by a theory of induction. Such a correlation is always a deliberate act of fallible intuition. Einstein stressed repeatedly the logical independence of concepts and sense impressions. On one particular occasion he did so with the following characteristically vivid humour. "The relation (of concepts and sense impressions) is not that of soup to beef but rather of wardrobe number to overcoat."[154] As Holton emphasized, the Einsteinian view of thinking as free play with concepts simultaneously highlights the role of creativity and the risks of delusion and fantasy.[155] This mixed blessing arises because the latter are dependent on exactly the same elements of thinking as the former. Of course, Einstein himself had underscored the tentative nature of the differentiation between sense impressions and representations. "(It) is not possible; or, at least, it is not possible with absolute certainty."[156]

With no rule to tell them the next step in research, scientists must decide for themselves what is reasonable doubt and bold intuition. Research scientists are more or less in situations similar to the one in which the mischievous physicist Carl Bosch once placed a newspaper correspondent.[157] The window of the laboratory where Bosch worked as a research student overlooked a block of flats. Giving free reign to his scientific curiosity, Bosch found his unsuspecting victim in a flat with a telephone in full view from the laboratory. Bosch phoned him and introduced himself as his own professor. He announced that he had perfected a new television device which enabled the user to see the speaker at the other end of the phone. The pressman was incredulous, but Bosch offered to give a demonstration. He invited the newspaper correspondent to adopt a series of postures, and then described them accurately. The result of this deception was an article in the next day's paper. There followed a bewildered verbal exchange between the victim and the real professor. The research scientist is always poised, so to speak, to play similar tricks on himself.

From the very beginnings of modern science, scientists have had to be forcefully reminded of the ever-sounding sirens of conceptual complacency. Recurrently, well-rehearsed performances mesmerize scientists until they founder on contact with reality. Classic cases from the annals of science's history include the absolute authority bestowed on the Ptolemaic system, Euclidean geometry, Newton's laws of motion and the indivisibility of the atom. Born commented on one example, "(Euclidean geometry) first showed that objects in the external world follow strict laws as regards their spatial properties. Later, delight in the beauty of these laws had the result that the empirical foundations of geometrical science were disregarded or even denied, and the study of its logical framework became an end in itself."[158]

An amusing tale told of the theoretician P. A. M. Dirac, supposedly while he was still a student, exaggerates the point.[159] Allegedly, Dirac attended a mathematical congress at which he was presented with the following problem. Three fishermen were so preoccupied with their unaccustomed success that they found themselves in darkness on a secluded island. Agreeing to spend the night on the island, each settled beside his boat. Two men were soon fast asleep, but one was unable to sleep. He decided to go home. Rather than disturb his companions, he threw the extra fish into the sea and divided the rest into three equal parts. He departed with his share of the catch.

About two hours later, a second fisherman awoke. Noiselessly he prepared to leave. He tossed the extra fish along the beach and divided the remaining fish into three equal parts, without realising that his friend had already gone. He too set off with his fish for the mainland. When the third fisherman arose, it was nearly morning though still dark. Unaware of the activities of his companions, he dumped the extra fish in the sea and divided the other fish into three equal piles. Pleased with his spoils, he also left the island quietly.

Dirac was asked to determine the least number of fish that the fishermen could have had. He proposed that there were initially (-2) fishes. The first fisherman threw one away leaving $(-2)-1 = (-3)$ fishes. He took (-1) with him, leaving $(-3) - (-1) = (-2)$ fishes. The second and third fishermen did exactly the same. When asked to solve this particular problem, Dirac is reputed to have responded in a characteristically "anti-social" way.

This is, of course, a delightful flight of fantasy about the scientist who fished the positive electron – the positron – out of the sea of electrons. It illustrates both the foolishness of solving a problem as an end in itself and the absurdity of losing contact with reality. It also exposes the inadequacy of Popper's view that only operations dictated by an algorithm are rational.[139] On the contrary, in accordance with an algorithm and violating no laws of logic, the unknown author of this tale obtained an irrational solution to the problem. Most practising scientists have painfully experienced the difference between faulty logic and irrationality in science.

Einstein's recognition of the recurrent neglect of the ambivalence of scientific theories was faithfully recounted by Lenzen. "Concepts that have proved useful in the constitution of an order of things readily win such an authority over us that we forget their earthly origin and take them as changeless data."[160] In fact, this is a quotation from Einstein's eulogy of Mach, published in 1916. It continued, "Then they become 'necessities of thought', 'given a priori', etc. The path of scientific progress is then, by such errors, barred for a long time. It is therefore no useless game if we are insisting on analyzing current notions and pointing out on what conditions their justification and usefulness depend, especially how they have grown from the data of experience. In this way their exaggerated authority is broken. They are removed, if they cannot properly legitimate themselves; corrected, if their correspondence to the given things was too negligently established; replaced by others, if a new system can be developed that we prefer for good reasons."[161]

Clearly, Einstein and those who appreciated the experimental grounds of his instructive insights saw the need to remain mindful of the ever-present dangers of scientific conservatism. By allowing the definable and operational characteristics of concepts and their relations to suppress, or effectively eliminate, the heuristic qualities of those concepts, scientists can develop a false sense of security. In other words, the logical ordering of sense impressions always threatens the free creations of the scientific mind. Familiarity with the success of existing rules and theories tends to breed contempt for their constructive origins. This contempt, in its turn, inhibits greatly the acceptance and the advancement of non-arbitrary, non-falsifiable, non-verifiable hypotheses.[162] Einstein realized that while theories are created by scientists, these inventions can come alive, turn upon their creators, and coerce them, and therefore their experiments, to conform to the resulting biologies.

Many scientists can surely be forgiven for assuming that Thomas S. Kuhn has transfigured Einstein's ideas into a retrospective classification for an analysis of science's history. Kuhn describes scientific research either as periods of scientific revolution involving new "paradigms" or explanations, or as periods of "normal" science characterized by an inattentiveness to "paradigmatic" foundations.[163] "Normal" or paradigmatic science addresses itself to "puzzles" because they are known to be solvable in principle, whereas "revolutionary" science accompanies the acknowledged failure of an entrenched paradigm to account for significant phenomena. This classification cannot cope, for instance, with the complex issues of the contributions of Poincaré, Lorentz and Einstein to the special theory of relativity. Nevertheless, the basic correspondence with Einstein's original thoughts is clear. Einstein, however, related in terms of scientific reorientations. He was careful not to obscure the dominant continuity of modern science with talk of scientific revolutions. For Einstein, the working scientist, continuity is rooted in the intuitive relation as are the free conceptual constructions of a general theory or "paradigm." However, what is referred to as "normal" science by Kuhn was a resurgence of debilitating authoritarianism in Einstein's view.

Scientists fashion, often unwittingly, their apprehensions of reality with habitual beliefs or routine assumptions. They visit them on the situations they confront. For instance, Newton's first law is untestable and remained effectively unchallenged for centuries until Einstein's powerful intellect penetrated its intrinsic ambiguity. He adapted this law in the light of the equivalence of gravitational and inertial masses. Inertial mass represents the reluctance of a particle to acceleration and gravitational mass its tendency to be pulled by another mass.[164]

A related hazard is the temptation to reduce reality to the sum of constructive constituents. This illusion prevents scientists from seeing beyond their models to the given rationality of the universe. According to Einstein, the pursuit of science relies heavily on the attitudes of scientists towards their hypotheses. Scientific advance depends on the commitment of scientists to the search for a greater logical unity. This search can uncover "paradigmatic" clues either in the course of essentially routine, basically unspectacular and logically consistent scientific researches, or during a premeditated attack on the foundations of a general theory. Outstanding examples are Planck's classical investigations of black body radiation and Einstein's early researches published in 1905, respectively. Einstein's intimate knowledge of quantum mechanics and the theories of relativity had convinced him of the presence of undiscovered dynamic order in nature. Consequently, he could neither associate himself with reductionism nor abandon causality to blind chance and static necessity. One of his inimitable sayings condensed his thoughts. "God is not playing dice."[165]

As already indicated, science seems to be ultimately a matter of faith. Scientists believe in the intelligibility of the universe and hope to discover aspects of it. Bluntly, their researches rely on reality impinging on them through intuition and carrying them into a new manifold. In plain language, Einstein rejected abstraction ultimately on the basis of conviction. When faced with the criticism that the complexity of scientific concepts masks the logical relation of concepts and reality, Einstein had to revert to his faith in the correlation of mind and matter. "The successes reaped up to now by science do, it is true, give a certain encouragement for this faith."[154] "It is the aim of science to establish general rules which determine the reciprocal connection of objects and events in time and space. For these rules, or laws of nature, absolutely general validity is required – not proven. It is mainly a program, and faith in the possibility of its accomplishment in principle is only founded on partial successes."[166] Science also "seeks to reduce the connections discovered to the smallest possible number of mutually independent conceptual elements. It is in this striving after the rational unification of the manifold that it encounters its greatest successes, even though it is precisely this attempt which causes it to run the greatest risk of falling a prey to illusions."[167]

In the final analysis, "a system has a truth-content according to the certainty and completeness of its co-ordination-possibility to the totality of experience."[168] With his deep conviction of the rationality of the universe, it seems that Einstein's "nose" for truth was far more precious to him than any presumptuous claims to "truth." In fact, Einstein could not attach a precise meaning to the term "scientific truth." Nevertheless, he "believed that scientific research can reduce superstition by encouraging people to think and view things in terms of cause and effect."[169] "As for the search for truth," wrote Einstein, "I know from my own painful searching, with its many blind alleys, how hard it is to take a reliable step, be it ever so small, towards the understanding of that which is truly significant."[170] According to Einstein, scientists discover the truth-contents of scientific theories by relying on faith and action to unmask delusion and fantasy.

12. POSSIBLE THEOLOGICAL CONNECTIONS

When seen against this brief outline of Einstein's views on scientific thinking, his occasional utterances reminiscent of biblical statements appear less enigmatic. Any mist around remarks like "only a life lived for others is a life worthwhile,"[171] "the true value of a human being is determined primarily by the measure and the sense in which he has attained liberation from the self,"[172] or "the creations of our mind shall be a blessing and not a curse to mankind"[171], begins to clear. Besides, such comments presuppose a broader context for the unrelenting strivings of individual scientists.

Although Einstein, like the vast majority of scientists, never formulated a rigorous metaphysics, he knew only too well that, in so far as scientists use reason, they can be said to embark on the philosophical enterprise. If they refuse to acknowledge this, they increase the risk of falling into severe contradiction. Einstein realised that modern science could not avoid philosophy. In fact, he saw the available explicit and implicit philosophies of scientists as reducible to two fundamental types. The first, the ontologistic, is characterised by an emphasis on the logical elements of science. It is based upon an underlying identity between scientist and nature. The second, the cosmological, concentrates on empirical aspects of science. It is commonly represented by positivism, and assumes the discrete co-existence of scientist and nature.

While it is fairly common knowledge that, at some stage or another, Einstein rejected Mach's philosophy as untenable, his dissatisfaction with the ontologistic type is less generally recognised. Indeed, on occasions, Einstein's views have been associated with the ontologism which suits Oriental religions. Actually, Einstein implied that each of the two types of philosophy provides a metaphysical basis for some aspects of modern science, but that each also precludes other equally important characteristics.

Oriental mystics are engaged in the quest for knowledge in the sense of immediate certainty. Einstein regarded scientific knowledge as mediated through sense impressions and intuitive faculties. He also saw the concomitant dangers of delusion and fantasy. In short, he reasoned that the possibility of error in scientific research precludes certainty. Hence the immediacy demanded by the mystic cannot be attained through the scientific enterprise. From an Einsteinian perspective, the fundamental issue appears to be: What do scientists accept as their criterion of the real – logic, experience or something else? The ontologistic position sees the denial of the supremacy of logic as a threat to all thinking and communication. Logic, therefore, is taken as normative for reality. By attempting to dictate to reality, the ontologistic approach fails to provide an adequate metaphysical framework for Einstein's views of modern scientific research.

According to Einstein, a "firm belief, a belief bound up with deep feelings, in a superior mind that reveals itself in the world of experience, represents (his) conception of God."[169] Knowledge of God, therefore, is not immediate but communicated by nature. Moreover, the relation of the scientist to God is inseparable from his relation to his colleagues. It is a triadic relationship. "In science . . . the work of the individual is so bound up with that of his scientific predecessors and contemporaries that it appears almost as an impersonal product of his generation."[173] The scientist does not long to become identical with nature or God. Indeed, there is an eternal inequality. "A finely tempered nature longs to escape from personal life into the world of objective perception and thought . . ."[70] Einstein believed that reality is invariant, that a real external world exists to be discovered by scientific research. "The contemplation of this world beckoned like a liberation, and (Einstein) soon noticed that many a man whom (he) had learned to esteem and to admire has found inner freedom and security in devoted occupation with it."[112]

By discovering the rational structure of the universe, the scientist discovers God himself but Einstein qualified this assertion repeatedly. The scientist's "religious feeling takes the form of a rapturous amazement at the harmony of natural law, which reveals an intelligence of such superiority that, compared with it, all the systematic thinking and acting of human beings is an utterly insignificant reflection."[174] Also, "whoever has undergone the intense experience of successful advances in this domain [science] is moved by profound reverence for the rationality made manifest in existence. By way of the undertaking he achieves a far reaching emancipation from the shackles of personal hopes and desires and thereby attains the humble attitude of mind toward the grandeur of reason incarnate in existence, and which, in its profoundest depths, is inaccessible to man. This attitude, however, appears to me [Einstein] to be religious, in the highest sense of the word."[167] Einstein was firmly convinced that scientific research involves a relation *between* God and scientist. This relation presupposes the plurality which the mystical or unitive ontologistic approach seeks to overcome.

For Einstein, scientific wisdom is conditioned by the commitment of the scientist. In contrast to the ontologistic way, his "eternal longing for understanding"[175] and his "ever-firm belief in the harmony of our world"[175] motivate him. Hence scientific knowledge is not primary. "Behind every achievement exists a motivation which is at the foundation of it . . ."[176] Clearly, the inadequacies were too numerous for the ontologistic approach to be espoused by Einstein. Consequently, having also rejected positivism, Einstein had to find a third type of philosophy.

The pre-established harmony between thought and reality provides for an intuitive relation between the private thinking and seeking of scientists and the world at large. This relation accommodates the influential spectra of physical, biological, cultural and spiritual events. The latter are cogent through the associations, preconceptions, commitments and emotions of every scientist.[177]

Einstein saw the inquiring, searching and probing scientist as individually open through intuition to the rationality of the universe or the whole of the natural order. Christians, or at least some of them, believe that the asking, seeking, and knocking Christian is personally open through the Holy Spirit to the Word of God by whom all things were made. He is open, therefore, to the entirety of the divinely created order. From an Einsteinian perspective it would appear that theological and scientific thinking might have epistemological points of contact. Indeed, if a suitable interaction model were found, such apparent parallelisms might provide a way in which science and theology could be mutually enriching. However, the development of science has repeatedly shown that false paths can be followed by mistaking analogy for evidence. The validity of such parallelisms should be established before they are taken too seriously.

Objectivity is certainly the hallmark of published scientific theories and data. Still, scientists are free to identify with whatever and whoever assists them in their theorizing and experimentation. In reality "hard experimental tests combine with the intellectual discontent, intellectual movement, intellectual attitudes of the moment. Certain kinds of theory, certain kinds of explanations, are then considered acceptable, and others are not considered acceptable."[178] Contrary to popular opinion, scientists are not depersonalized by scientific research. Modern science is a human activity on which the whole gamut of human experiences have a bearing. Nevertheless, scientists are always guided by and subject to the immediate intimations of the rationality of the natural order.[154] "Every scientist, in working out his own research, gravitates to particular points on the boundary which separates the known from the unknown, and becomes inclined to take his particular perspective from these points."[179] The scientist's personally chosen expertise, provides him with the necessary specificity to engage uniquely in the general quest for scientific knowledge. Expressed differently, the scientist's personal perspective on scientific knowledge, as Einstein conceived it, takes into account the totality of presuppositions which represent his claims to knowledge. His private scientific thinking stems from his personal involvement or calling to serve in "the temple of science."[180] In other words, scientific "personalities are not formed by what is heard or said, but by labour and activity."[181]

Einstein was acutely conscious of the indispensability of the individual liberty of scientists. To reject this freedom, or to ignore it, is to introduce a very dangerous dichotomy. The latter invites the relegation of discovery to realms of irrationality. It also encourages the recasting of scientific statements into statements without empirical foundation. Scientific thinking is thinking of, and on the basis of, the given reality of the rational universe. It is valid only in so far as it derives from that rationality and refers back to it. This two-fold reference is achieved through the free individual labour and activity of scientists.

Many Christians are correspondingly sensitive to the theological significance of the personal freedom of the Christian. To infringe this God-given privilege, or to surrender it, is to identify with disjunctive disobedience. The latter degenerates life to anarchic chaos and culminates in death. It also degrades theological statements to statements without conformity to the self-communication of the Word of God. Theological thinking is thinking of, and grounded in, the Reality of the economic condescension of God. This means that the Eternal Word, without ceasing to be Word, has accommodated himself to humankind in its weaknesses and incapacities in order to effect communion. Theological thinking is authentic only in so far as it respires that Word and aspires to his sacrifical communication. This dual identification is accomplished through the free personal worship and mission of the Christian. The intriguing fact is that such alluring parallels between scientific and theological thinking can be sketched so readily. It suggests that a greater familiarity with the nature of scientific thinking might benefit Christians, if only to allow them to distinguish more effectively between the two.

Einstein's emphasis on the difference between private scientific thinking and public scientific knowledge requires a qualitative differentiation between scientific wisdom and scientific information, between assimilation and acquisition. He was convinced that "if a person masters the fundamentals of his subject and has learned to think and work independently, he will surely find his way and besides will be better able to adapt himself to progress and changes than the person whose training principally consists in the acquiring of detailed knowledge."[182] Scientists with first-hand apprehension of their disciplines are capable of deliberating on the relevant issues. People who lack this wisdom are not competent to make scientific decisions. Scientific judgements of significance and coherence can be made only within a scientific game. Persons who, so to speak, have not played the game, are obviously incapable of arriving at scientific conclusions. Harold Brown's description of rationality is not new.[183] Indeed, it bears a striking resemblance to views expressed by Einstein well over forty years ago.

It is very easy for scientists to acquire so many facts, so much data, that they swamp their powers of assimilation. They also have ample opportunity to apply particular theories in a variety of ways without necessarily coming to grips with their fundamental principles. Indeed, on one occasion, Einstein criticized severely an eminent fellow scientist saying of him that he "couldn't really understand how anybody could know so much and understand so little."[184] Learning the facts and memorizing the theories can never compete with learning the theories and memorizing the facts. Only the latter can develop a keen sense of scientific direction.

There are usually mitigating circumstances. "It is, in fact, very common in physical investigation," wrote Born, "to find it easier to derive a formal relation from extensive observational material than to understand its real significance. The reason for this lies deep in the nature of physical experience; the world of physical objects lies outside the realm of the senses and of observation, which only border on it; and it is difficult to illuminate the interior of an extensive region from its boundaries."[185] On the other hand, Born had strong words for offenders of a different persuasion. "A theoretician who, immersed in his formulae, forgets the phenomena which he wants to explain is no real scientist, physicist or chemist, and if he is estranged by his books from the beauty and variety of nature I would call him a poor fool."[186]

The physicist Lewis Branscomb described a related incident in the working life of Vladimir Rojansky.[187] Rojansky was asked to interpret the experimental results of a fellow physicist. Two weeks passed before the experimentalist inquired about Rojansky's progress. "I've almost solved the problem," said Rojansky, "but give me another week. I'm having trouble explaining the high temperature behaviour." In awe of the theoretician the experimentalist showed patience. A few days later, Rojansky appeared with the fruit of his labours. His ingenious theoretical prediction went right through all of the experimental points, including the troublesome one in the lower right-hand corner. "It was easy to explain the steady rise with temperature," Rojansky reported, "but I had a terrible time understanding the phenomenon that turns the curve over so suddenly at that last point." "But that point," gasped the experimentalist, "is part of the legend!" To be fair to Rojansky, it should be stressed that this incident arose out of a simple misunderstanding rather than any wilful estrangement from nature on his part. Nevertheless, as both scientists knew, the resulting formulae had no bearing on reality.

Christians are well aware of those who have ears to hear and eyes to see but who do neither. Perhaps some of them cannot because of the erratic contrivances of modern biblical scholarship. The inexhaustible extra-biblical solutions that could be used to appease the imagination of the scholar present formidable problems. They promise to reduce biblical content to infinite dilution in the absence of an appropriate principle of relevance. The accumulation of information from "comparative" sources, "identified literary" sources, "conventional" forms, hypothetical "oral traditions," and philological and etymological studies is not equivalent to the growth of understanding. From this swelling tide of data it is too easy to fish "anti-theological" creations which illustrate the foolishness of speculative self-indulgence. Without some cognizance of the intrinsic rationality common to all biblical sources, the acquisition of information using diverse theological accoutrements inhibits assimilation. Modern biblical techniques remain entirely arbitrary until their underlying assumptions are grounded in some higher rationality. Without this grounding those procedures have little in common with modern science. It is, therefore, dangerously misleading to refer to them collectively as "critical science." To avoid sheer mechanical manipulation, biblical techniques should always be placed in an adequate theological context of which they are only necessary parts. It should also be noted that, when theological contexts or Christian dogmatics become autonomous, they too have been reduced to mechanical contraptions.

Evidently scientific and theological thinking are susceptible to similar seditions. While science is currently confused with technology, theology is presently bemused by the techniques of biblical studies. Baseless speculation and a logic of contriving threaten both modern science and Christian theology. Einstein, the physicist, knew that "for us human beings, our mutual behaviour and our conscious strivings for our goals are much more important than any factual knowledge."[171] Thinking scientifically involves assessments on the basis of relevant scientific evidence. The demand to be scientific obligates scientists to search for scientific grounds on which they can make scientific decisions. Thinking theologically presumably consists of somewhat similar aspirations.

The perspicuity and perspicacity that are attested by Einstein's scientific work are equally affirmed by his epistemological utterances. They are also confirmed by almost everyone who met him. They are franked by courage and unconventionality. The essence of Einstein's wisdom lay in his childlike simplicity to think things that many others had thought many times before him, but to think them in entirely new connections. For example, everybody had known for about seventy years that the law of electromagnetic

induction depended on relative motion. Nobody had been sufficiently bothered by the fact that the theory did not take this
circumstance into account.[188] Einstein was the exception who
arrived at the special theory of relativity. Again, the knowledge that
inertial and gravitational masses are equal, the principle of equivalence, had been known for about two hundred and fifty years. By
brooding over this principle, Einstein was able to build the general
theory of relativity.[189]

Clearly, scratching the surface of Einstein's "occasional utterances of an epistomological content"[189] is sufficient to reveal the
possibility of connections between scientific and theological thinking. However, before one can pursue those matters, one must have
some notion of how and why Einstein "trie(d) to make for himself
in the fashion that suit(ed) him best a simplified and intelligible
picture of the world."[70] As he himself said, "Behind every
achievement exists a motivation which is at the foundation of it and
which in turn is strengthened and nourished by the accomplishment of the undertaking."[190] Obviously, a discussion of some
aspects of Einstein's achievements is advisable before their origins
are considered.

13. GOOD REASONS

Many Christians will probably concede that even a bird's-eye view
of the development of Einstein's scientific researches is worth the
effort for its own sake. Most of them are likely to resist the
suggestion that it is particularly meaningful to Christians interested
in the general nature of scientific thinking. Indeed, many of their
expressed opinions and their expedient references bear witness to
the strength of this resistance. Moreoever, Einstein himself admitted that scientists are essentially "uncommunicative solitary fellows." Does it make any sense then for Christians to consider in
detail selected aspects of one specific case? Actually there are several
reasons why this task merits attention, despite the probability that it
will shoot far more questions than it can possibly bag.

First, Albert Einstein was not an ordinary Nobel laureate. His
scientific achievement has made it "inconceivable that there will be
any general reversion to pre-Copernican, pre-Newtonian or pre-
Darwinian assumptions concerning the general nature of the universe and man's place in it(.T)here will likewise be no return to the

world-view of Einstein's predecessors."[191] Einstein's scientific contributions challenged humankind by presenting it with a whole variety of options. When taken up, they changed the course of human history. Modern Christians can only benefit from a clearer understanding of the important distinction between Einstein's achievement and humankind's applications of it. One way to seek such clarity is to glean direct from Einstein's work a little about the personality and modes of thought behind it.

Second, a cursory inspection of the principal connections between one brief phase of Einstein's researches and the contemporary public scientific knowledge demonstrates that continuous scientific development undergirds local methodological discontinuities.[192] Such an appraisal raises doubts about what some philosophers and historians of science refer to as "scientific revolutions." It also highlights the conservative, instructive and regulative roles of scientific learning.

Third, Einstein's scientific researches show the great power of the intuitive relation, especially when placed in a semblance of the concrete where, when, and from whom he assimilated heuristic concepts. In particular, they demonstrate that the "labour and activity" of the individual scientist is of far greater consequence for understanding scientific research than preconceived notions of a simple standardized scientific method.

The opposite extreme, of course, is to describe modern scientific research as anarchic or irrational. There are powerful inducements to lapse into subjectivism. Deceptively, some of the most profound and creative scientific researches were accomplished by individuals who responded to the singular circumstances of distinctly personal experiences. In a half-waking dream Friedrich August Kékulé saw a snake eating its own tail as his original conception of the formation of molecules of benzene and its derivatives. The snake became chains of carbon atoms coiled into hexagonal rings.[193] Presented in 1865, this description was accepted by most chemists long before modern theories of chemical valence explained the stability of aromatic compounds. It seems that a hypnagogic state and a strong conviction conspired to advance stereochemistry.

In 1911 Ernest Rutherford's students presented him with some astonishing but convincing evidence. It proved that an occasional α-particle emitted from a parent radium atom rebounded backwards from its metallic foil target.[194] Collision with an electron could not account for this unexpected phenomenon. The α-particle is thousands of times more massive than an electron. Rutherford's vivid imagery captures that moment. "It was almost as incredible as if you had fired a 15-inch shell at a piece of tissue paper and it had come back and hit you."[195] On the basis of available theories of statistics, those results seemed to be beyond belief. Boldly, Rutherford interpreted them as indicating that the structure of the atom resembled that of the solar system. He concluded that the atom's central tiny heavy nucleus was surrounded by electrons traversing the vast emptiness of atomic space and went off to learn the mathematics. Apparently, a combination of serendipity and imaginative brilliance associated the infinitely large and small to provide the rudiments of modern atomic theory.

In 1935 Hideki Yukawa suggested his meson theory of nuclear forces. He developed it from a nuclear model based on the structure of the atom. Yukawa postulated for the proton–neutron pair a parallel to the continuous quantal exchange of the nucleus–electron pair.[196] This required the existence of a new kind of particle, called the meson. Its mass, if charged, would be intermediate between those of the electron and proton. In 1936 Carl David Anderson made the first observation of such a particle. It appears that a fantastic flash of intuitive insight led to the first rational account of nuclear binding forces.

The sequels to a chemist dozing in his armchair by the fire, happy accidents in the laboratory of an experimental enthusiast, and the intuitive hunch of a theoretical physicist were seminal developments in organic chemistry, atomic theory, and sub-nuclear physics, respectively. Frustratingly, many scientists doze but do not, thereby, discover. Few of the millions of accidents in the scientific laboratories have happy endings. Even more rarely do intuitive hunches pay such large and immediate dividends. Nevertheless, these are the things Nobel laureates are made of, or so some would have Christians believe.

A closer look at only four of Einstein's scientific publications will alert open-minded Christians to the grave distortions that can result from scant descriptions of the fruits of decades of personal scientific learning, labour, and commitment. Although the transitional point from a scientific problem to its solution may be signalled by an exceptional personal experience, this is not invariably the case. To isolate this type of event as the crucial factor in scientific discovery is to respond, naively, to scientific results. It is reasonable to assume that such transitions indicate the presence of an intuitive component in scientific thinking. The frequency of their occurrences does not automatically justify, however, interventionist interpretations of scientific creativity.

Those, then, are a few important reasons why Christians should learn something of the salient features of the development of the Einstein's scientific researches. But most significantly, by doing so they will prepare the ground for a realistic appreciation of modern scientific thinking. However, the benefits of brooding are only seen at hatching.

14. SCIENTIFIC CONTINUITY

In 1905 Einstein published in *Annalen der Physik* four papers that accelerated markedly the advance of the natural sciences. Each paper included the solution to a major scientific problem. However, as Einstein pointed out, all four contributions were products of his general preoccupation with "the electro-magnetic foundations of physics."[197] Born's apposite aphorism is, "Einstein's conception of the physical world cannot be divided into watertight compartments."[198]

In the earliest of these papers Einstein considered the current differing theoretical treatments of the discontinuous nature of gases and other ponderable bodies and their energies, on the one hand, and of the continuous character of electromagnetic processes in "empty space," on the other.[199] Toward its end he discussed the anomalous photoelectric effect which had been a stone in the scientific shoe for many years. Heinrich Rudolf Hertz had discovered that certain metals in a high vacuum emitted electrons on irradiation with ultra-violet light (the photoelectric effect).[200] Subsequently, Philip Lenard had investigated this effect. He obtained experimental results in sharp contrast with expectations based on Maxwell's theory. Three years later in 1905, Lenard was awarded the Nobel Prize and Einstein provided an explanation of the puzzling experimental data.

The wave theory of light predicts that "a certain definite proportion of the energy of radiation is transformed into energy of motion of the electrons."[201] It also requires "the velocity of the emitted electrons to increase if the intensity of the light increases."[201] The experimental results indicated that the energy of the emitted electron is independent of the intensity of the light. Moreover, they showed that its energy decreases proportionally as the wavelength increases. "The remarkable thing about the process is that only the number, and not the velocity, of the electrons emitted depends on the intensity of the light. The wave picture of light is of no use in understanding this: for, if we move the metal plate away from the light source, the incident wave becomes weaker and more and more rarified, and it is incomprehensible how it can always communicate the same energy to an electron."[202]

In his treatment of this effect Einstein showed that the experimental evidence is consistent with a description of the radiation as a stream of minute particles, quanta or photons. Intuitively, he adapted the ideas of Max Planck who had used discreteness of energy to resolve the problem later referred to as the Ultra-violet Catastrophe. By explaining the photoelectric effect in this fashion, Einstein illustrated the heuristic power of the quantum hypothesis. Only in the following year did he realize that Planck had also introduced discreteness into the physics of charged harmonic oscillators.[203] In particular, Planck's work concerned the emission and absorption of light, not the structure of the radiation itself. It represented the origin of quantum theory, whereas Einstein's contribution signalled the development of quantum theory. The latter was acknowledged as such by the Nobel prize committee in its award to him. Einstein had absorbed Planck's theoretical construct, produced a conceptual variant, and applied it to the anomalous phenomenon discovered by Hertz and investigated by Lenard.

Actually, Einstein did not use Planck's radiation law. He argued correctly that the earlier and simpler law of Wilhelm Wien represents the limiting case for low radiation density. Under the latter conditions, the corpuscular character of the radiation is more evident.[204] Einstein ascribed discontinuities to the emitted energy, whereas Planck had done so only to the emitter. Nevertheless, it is abundantly clear that the common interests of all five scientists were the properties of electromagnetic radiation and the area of applicability of Maxwell's theory.

In 1856 the young physicist James Clerk Maxwell had developed a mathematical description of Michael Faraday's intuitive ideas of the "field." In doing so he had unified electricity, magnetism and optics.[205] Maxwell's equations did not include even the basic equations of Newton's theory. Still they accounted for numerous and diverse phenomena, so much so that their explanatory power as a fundamental theory rapidly and seriously rivalled that of Newton's theory. As Einstein and Infeld stated, "The formulation of (Maxwell's) equations is the most important event in physics since Newton's time, not only because of their wealth of content, but also because they form a pattern for a new type of law. The characteristic features of Maxwell's equations, appearing in all other equations of modern physics, are summarized in one sentence. Maxwell's equations are laws representing the *structure* of the field."[206]

In immediate practical terms, Maxwell's theory had indicated that visible light waves represent only a small part of a vast range of electromagnetic processes. The discovery of infra-red and ultraviolet radiation encouraged the search for hitherto unobserved forms of electromagnetic radiation. By 1886 Hertz had generated and detected radio waves and demonstrated their diffraction, interference and polarization effects.[200] Characteristic of the self-correcting heuristics of science, this work led to the discovery of the photoelectric effect. More generally, it revealed that Maxwell's theory had raised its own brace of anomalies.[207]

Against this scientific background, Einstein's interest in the wave-particle duality appears eminently rational. This duality epitomized the confrontation between Newtonian and Maxwellian physics. A robust platform of scientific development allowed Einstein to pioneer this particular field. He learned from the explorations of others, maintained established links in the conceptual chain, and secured new connections in theoretically and experimentally familiar ground. His paper pointed scientific investigation beyond itself toward greater precision and fuller apprehension.

In another contribution to *Annalen der Physik* in 1905, Einstein dealt with the applicability of statistical mechanics to microscopically observable phenomena.[208] Three years earlier, he had extended the work of Ludwig Bolzmann. His efforts amounted to "a rediscovery of all the essential features of statistical mechanics" as thoroughly and independently treated by Josiah Willard Gibbs the previous year.[209] Einstein had then proceeded to an analysis of the random motion of a small particle suspended in a fluid. He assumed that such a particle is continually bombarded by molecules conforming to a statistical mechanical description. This assumption enabled him to derive an expression for the magnitude of molecular dimensions in terms of experimentally determinable quantities. Significantly, Einstein predicted an observable effect and tentatively correlated it with what had been observed as Brownian motion.[197]

His hesitancy reflected a meagre knowledge of that kind of motion.

The naturalist Robert Brown had observed seventy years earlier the zigzag motion of minute pollen grains or inorganic dust particles suspended in a fluid. This type of motion, named after him, was not caused by any external influence. It remained unexplained until Einstein accounted for it on the basis of his molecular and statistical hypotheses. The "fundamental step taken by Einstein," Born stressed, "was the idea of raising the kinetic theory of matter from a possible plausible hypothesis to a matter of observation, by pointing out cases where the molecular motion and its statistical character can be made visible."[210]

In more than one sense, Einstein's researches followed the activities of Maxwell. Neither scientist confined his attention to electromagnetic theory.[211] Maxwell was the first to apply the idea of probability to the seventeenth century creation, the kinetic theory. According to this notion, a gas is composed of vast numbers of tiny particles speeding around in all directions. They collide with one another and bounce off the surfaces of their containing vessel. From this invisible chaos Maxwell extracted order. He showed that the distribution of energy among the particles can be calculated precisely because the motions, collisions and bombardments of the particles are random. The outstanding feature of his mathematical description is its independence of the detailed nature of both the particles and the forces they exert on each other. His treatment pointed to a fundamental property of matter in equilibrium. This concept flamed the intuition of scientists like Boltzmann, Gibbs and Einstein. In particular, Boltzmann interpreted the Second Law of Thermodynamics in terms of probability, and as already noted, both Gibbs and Einstein developed aspects of the former's pioneering work.

Einstein's treatment of Brownian motion along with Planck's earlier determination of molecular size from radiation studies convinced most sceptical scientists of the reality of atoms and molecules. Once again, its dependence on, relevance to and continuation of, prior scientific studies encouraged scientists to regard this Einsteinian contribution as a sizable local movement of science which is continually bombarded by new theoretical and methodological entities.

A third paper presented the now-familiar special theory of relativity. Its title On the Electrodynamics of Moving Bodies indicates that it arose out of the same scientific milieu.[212] In fact, Einstein explained the close association of ideas.[213] The small particle suspended in a fluid became a "freely moving, quasi-monochromatically reflecting mirror" in a space filled with radiation. The bombarding molecules became bombarding quanta of radiation. The photoelectric effect was seen as a typical example of the general wave-particle nature of microscopic phenomena. Newtonian theory could not cope with the time irreversibility of the Second Law of Thermodynamics or the wave-particle duality of electromagnetic radiation. Maxwell's theory could not account for the corpuscular nature of microscopic processes. A new unifying theory was needed.

After considerable time spent in despairing efforts to construct an alternative theory on the basis of the facts, Einstein eventually concluded that an analogy to the Second Law was required. He discovered one, but not without prolonged deliberation.[214] His appeal to the Second Law of Thermodynamics was based on an earlier discovery. This law applied to both electromagnetic radiation and ponderable particulate aggregates.[215] The Second Law was general in this respect. Therefore, it appeared more fundamental than either Maxwell's equations or Newtonian mechanics with its associated concepts of mass and force. There was nothing arbitrary about Einstein's thinking. On the contrary, it was firmly rooted in his private scientific experience of the continuous growth of public scientific knowledge.

From his reading of the philosophical writings of David Hume and the scientific writings of Ernst Mach, Einstein learned the value of critical reasoning, particularly of epistemological analysis.[216] Maxwell's equations predicted that the speed of light is finite and independent of both the source and the observer. In empty space the velocity of all electromagnetic waves is the same.[217] Those equations imply absolute rest in the sense that bodies "at rest" should behave differently from those in uniform motion. Specifically, a charged electrical condenser with parallel plates should rotate when moving, but not if at rest. Absolute rest meant at rest relative to the medium in which the light was transmitted. In his critique of the Newtonian theory of motion, Mach had returned to Newton's views on the kinematical irrelevance of absolute space and time.[218] Some change was needed, therefore, in order that Maxwell's equations, like Newton's, would apply in all inertial frames. Einstein proposed that the velocity of light was a fundamental invariant independent of the motion of the source and the observer. Therefore, the concept of a "light medium" or "luminiferous ether" was superfluous. Actually, as early as 1899 Jules Henre Poincaré had expressed doubts about both the existence of the ether and the detection of absolute motion.[219] But Einstein did not know of Poincaré's consecutive investigations.[220]

The measurement of motion depends on the measurement of time. The latter is based on the concept of simultaniety. This concept relies on the use of light signals. The conceptual key was Einstein's realization that the velocity of light is only practically infinite in daily life.[221] While the idea of the simultaneity of two events occurring in the same place is acceptable, the corresponding notion for two events at different locations presents problems.[221] In fact, it has no physical meaning. This led Einstein to "the recognition of the relativity of the concept of simultaneity."[222] If simultaneity is relative, so are distance, speed, acceleration, force, energy *etc*. In other words, the basis of the natural sciences is transformed.

By assuming that the laws of nature are independent of the choice of the inertial system, i.e., by extending the principle of relativity operative in Newtonian mechanics to all physical processes[223], Einstein arrived at "relations of a new type (Lorentz transformations) . . . for the conversion of co-ordinates and times of events." Einstein's desired "restricting principle for natural laws, comparable to the restricting principle of the non-existence of the *perpetuum mobile* which underlies mechanics," turned out to be that "(t)he laws of physics are invariant with respect to Lorentz-transformations (for the transition from one inertial system to any other arbitrarily chosen system of inertia)."[224] The principle of relativity does not assert, however, that all things are only relative. In fact, it requires that natural laws are determinate despite the reality that all observers do not experience the same effects. The private times and spaces of different observers do not exist in isolation. They all belong to a single objective public space-time called the universe. For Einstein, reality is invariant. A real external world exists which can be discovered through scientific research. The objective laws of nature are invariant in all frames of reference. By distinguishing the variant from the invariant scientists penetrate the dynamic structures of reality. They lose the notion of an extended rigid body but gain deeper apprehension of physical reality whose objectivity contrasts sharply with all forms of cultural relativism.

In this third paper Einstein derived the Lorentz transformations.

Unknown to him, an alternative derivation had been presented earlier by Hendrik Anton Lorentz.[225] Einstein's theory was, however, profoundly different. Lorentz had obtained his equations by using *ad hoc* assumptions to modify Newtonian theory.[226] The special theory of relativity was based on two fundamental postulates. Those conjectures were not arbitrary. They were firmly rooted in available scientific theories and observations.[227] Through them it was shown that the Lorentz transformations had universal validity. Einstein admitted freely that he had known of the earlier studies of Lorentz, but not of his later work (1904).[228] But as Einstein explained, the important new feature of his theory was the realization that the bearing of the Lorentz transformations transcended their connections with Maxwell's equations. It concerned the nature of space and time. Set against the knowledge that Maxwell's equations did not account for the microstructure of radiation (photoelectric effect etc.), this feature had particular significance for Einstein. It gave him somewhere to hang his hope of penetrating the underlying interdependence of all his researches.[228]

The Lorentz transformations reduce in the limit of small velocity to the familiar Galilean transformations. Similarly, the relativistic transformation of velocities reverts to classical form. The effects of length contraction, time dilation and velocity-dependent mass, all derivable from the Lorentz transformations, are integral aspects of Einstein's theory. This paper also contains a new theory of the Doppler shift, a new treatment of Bradley's aberration of light, and modified electromagnetic equations, based on Hertz's formulation, from which the law of conservation of charge can be derived. A new theory of motion of the electron including an outline of an experimental test represents the conclusion and the aim of this impressive contribution. As a charged ponderable body, the electron had to obey both a theory of mechanics and some form of electromagnetic theory. Einstein produced a unifying theory of the electrodynamics of moving bodies.

The fourth short paper spells out the now-famous proposal that all energy has mass as a novel consequence of the theory of relativity. It indicates a tentative correlation with observed properties of radium salts.[229] The realization that "radiation conveys inertia between the emitting and absorbing bodies"[230] points scientists beyond the old discrete-continuous disunities. Two years later, Einstein propounded the more important formula $E = mc^2$, which asserted that all mass is equivalent to energy. Thus, his short note of

1905 represented the first major step towards a deeper understanding of both the instability of radioactive atoms and the stability of the stars as they continue to radiate vast quantities of light and heat.

Consistently, all four papers reflect Einstein's great interest in theoretical particulars and his relative reticence about experimental details.[231] Those publications demonstrate his concern with fundamental principles. At times, they betray his ignorance of some recent scientific literature. It has to be remembered, of course, that they were conceived in effective isolation. As Ronald Clark put it, "(Einstein) had the run of the Patent Office library, strong on engineering but weak on physics, and he read the leading physics journals published in German. But he had access to little else. Neither did he work, nor could he talk and debate on social occasions, inside a university environment with its incessant point counter point of argument, its constant cross-fertilization of ideas and its stimulating climate of inquiry . . . thus from 1902 until 1905 Einstein worked on his own, an outsider of outsiders, scientifically provincial and having few links with the main body of contemporary physics."[232]

Nevertheless, there was nothing isolated about the scientific content of Einstein's researches. His explanation of the photoelectric effect was eventually recognized as the birth of quantum theory with Planck's innovation regarded as its conception. The Brownian motion was hailed in the light of Einstein's work as penultimate to the observation of atoms and molecules. The special theory of relativity, reducible to Newtonian theory in the limit of terrestrial velocities, reconciled kinematics and electromagnetism. It replaced the two logically independent concepts of electric vector field and magnetic vector field by a single tensor field. It also collapsed into one law the laws of matter, momentum and energy conservation. The attribution of mass to energy pointed the way to a fuller apprehension of atomic structure. Later, the equation of mass and energy provided a quantitative basis for the earlier work of Rutherford and others, who had already established through their studies of radioactive decay that the atom contained vast energy resources.[233]

Louis de Broglie has described Einstein's four papers as "blazing rockets which in the dark of the night suddenly cast a brief but powerful illumination over an immense unknown region."[234] All four publications planted the seeds of new scientific theories though Einstein did not care to nurse them unduly. Repeatedly, he outlined possibilities for experimental investigation, but paid little attention to practicalities. Einstein's papers published in 1905 were relevant to the work of Bradley, Boltzmann, Brown, Doppler, Fitzgerald, Helmholtz, Hertz, Jeans, Kirchhoff, Kohlrausch, Lenard, Lorentz, Mach, Maxwell, Michelson, Morley, Newton, Ostwald, Planck, Poincaré, Rayleigh, Riemann, Rutherford, Voigt, Weber and Wien to name only a few leading scientific lights. As already noted, Einstein himself declared that "in science . . . the work of the individual scientist is so bound up with that of his scientific predecessors and contemporaries that it appears almost as an impersonal product of his generation."[235] Prior converging lines of scientific research met in Einstein's work as the focal point. From it they emerged to illuminate a new diversity of phenomena amenable to scientific investigation. The hallmark on Einstein's achievement reads "science." The term "revolution" is totally inadequate.[236]

In 1928, Born emphasized the importance of continuity to scientific research. He discussed it in relation to Maxwell's equations, Fresnel's proof of diffraction, the theory of relativity and quantum mechanics.[237] Twenty three years later his conviction remained firm.[238] Bondi stressed repeatedly that the development of the special theory of relativity stands "four-square on Newton's first law of motion."[239] Almost thirty years ago, Holton commented, "The more urgent fact is that 'revolutionary' ideas arise only very rarely compared with the large number of workable or even great ideas conceived within the *traditional* setting, so that the individual scientist is wisely predisposed to favor the type of advance which he knows and believes in from personal experience."[240] Eight years later, he too re-affirmed his adherence to the theme of continuity. "The so-called scientific 'revolution' turns out to be at bottom an effort to return to classical purity. This is not only a key to a new evaluation of Einstein's contribution, but indicates a fairly general characteristic of great scientific 'revolutions'."[241]

15. COMMITMENT AND ACTION

Einstein's four papers had a powerfully heuristic impact on scientific development because it had first had an unrivalled influence on him. "At that time Einstein's gift for divining such correlations was almost uncanny." Born continued, "It was based on a (basically) thorough knowledge of experimental facts combined with a profound understanding of the present state of the theory, which enabled him to see at once where something strange was happening."[242] With so much learning under his belt, Einstein was sufficiently edified to look through and beyond its conservative, instructive and regulative roles.

The same can be said of Kékulé, Rutherford, and Yukawa, none of whom could have benefited from their distinctly personal experiences without the "labour and activity" so necessary to attune them to the harmonies of nature.[110] To select an example, Rutherford had already won the Nobel prize when he discovered the atomic nucleus. The prize had been awarded for his demonstration that naturally occurring radioactive atoms decay spontaneously into other atomic species. This achievement had encouraged chemists and physicists in their attempts to understand atomic structure. Continuing with his research on the atomic nucleus, Rutherford the Nobel laureate was the first to change one atomic species into another by artificial means. This sequence of closely related successes was once vexingly referred to by a friend who said to Rutherford, "You are a lucky man . . . Always on the crest of the wave!" The eminent researcher replied, "Well, I made the wave, didn't I . . ." Rutherford had not worked very hard on his modesty, but he had driven himself remorselessly for decades in search of "the theory of matter."[243]

Rutherford's commitment matched that of the finest scientists. What Einstein said of Johannes Kepler's commitment, for instance, on the occasion of the three hundredth anniversary of his death, is equally applicable to Rutherford's devotion. "How great must his [Kepler's] faith in the existence of natural law have been to give him the strength to devote decades of hard and patient work to the empirical investigation of planetary motion and the mathematical laws of that motion, entirely on his own, supported by no one and understood by very few!"[120] In general what scientists get out of their researches depends to a considerable extent on what they put into them. According to Einstein, facts are theory-laden and theories are empirically loaded. Achievements do not visit scientists like bolts out of the blue, although the manner of their appearances might suggest otherwise to non-scientific observers.

The cumulative, corporate nature of public science communicates to individual scientists through the intuitive relation its received intimations of the rationality of the universe. The research student's apprenticeship and his supervisor's associations with colleagues foster, but cannot guarantee, the transmission of a wide range of skill, information and wisdom. All are necessary in the continuous pursuit of science. The learning of an old theory or the discovery of a new one is simultaneously an irreversible heuristic enterprise and a reversible logical exercise. Their desires for greater logical clarity and unity transform scientists both intellectually and appetitively. They respond to hopes of refined contacts with reality, by entering conceptual hysteresis loops of scientific research. Thus, they expand their scientific apprehension and experience. Always they relate to the mystery of reality directly as individuals. Yet, to a considerable extent, they perform reflectively as members of the scientific community.

As scientists study the basic principles, and also the published literature, relevant to their subjects, they discipline themselves. They learn to do so by reappraising past developments and current reorientations within their specialisms. They strive continually to assimilate, to improve scientific wisdom, in order to be more capable of recognizing and pursuing original scientific insights.[97] Scientific genius seems to be the personal labour of setting one's fire with wood chopped by others and then lighting it with a match taken from a growing sympathy with the natural order. That sympathy thrives as long as scientists identify with the work of other scientists. Of course, they must react creatively to it. There is a sense in which the scientific genius possesses a deeper apprehension than the ordinary scientific researcher. This sense is not easy to specify. Certainly, it includes, among other things, a keener awareness of the implications of scientific theories and a wider range of scientific interests.

Actually, the Einsteinian view that scientific knowledge is not primary but depends on the commitment of the scientist places considerable emphasis on the severely underrated notion of scientific freedom. The modern scientific enterprise depends heavily on the decisions of its researchers. For example, they must decide for themselves the range of their interests, the nature of their specialisms, and the intensity and extent of their labours. Scientific researchers can neither act nor think without at least implying criteria of significance and coherence. The idea of a completely orderless scientific freedom precludes the possibility of such criteria. Hence, decision is eliminated and, therefore, scientific freedom is meaningless. Obviously, scientific freedom must be structured in some way if it is meaningful. The ordering of its structure must originate beyond the scientist himself. As far as Einstein could see, the rudimentary framework of a theory of scientific knowledge could not be formulated without some such external reference. The central question for him was: "What are acceptable scientific criteria of significance and coherence?"

Einstein avoided complete relativism in scientific knowledge because he believed in an external world independent of the observer.[128] The invariance of the laws of nature permits a multiplicity of scientific games or partial views of reality, while guaranteeing its superior rationality. The pre-established harmony between thought and reality enables the scientist to apprehend aspects of the natural order. As already noted, all knowledge of reality begins and ends in experience.[244] Sooner or later, all scientific theories are shown to be inadequate. In other words, delusion and fantasy are exposable by scientific experience because scientific theories have less freedom than the scientist himself.

In fact, the rationality of the universe is vastly superior to that of the individual scientist. Consequently, Einstein assessed scientific concepts and theories by their success in structuring the manifold of sense experience. He safeguarded the freedom of the scientific researcher by subordinating his decisions ultimately and exclusively to the natural order. In so far as a scientific theory is merely a tool in the hand of the scientist, both have entered, so to speak, into a compact of deceit. The scientist confers on the theory a false authority, and in return he receives an illicit sense of certainty. At some stage, this double-duplicity betrays the theory. The only kind of scientific theory that could invariably resist such complicity would be one with the freedom to oppose the scientist's decisions. Einstein believed that that scientific theory is the rationality of the universe and that the pre-established harmony between thought and reality is its means of expressing its resistance.

Einstein went much further. A decision is always made by someone, not by something. Besides, whatever evidence the scientist accepts, whether that of experience or that of logic, it will depend neither on experience nor on logic alone. All scientific knowledge is ultimately based on a decision in favour of one or the other or both. Scientific knowledge always presupposes the freedom of the scientist who makes a decision, even if it is to abandon the pursuit of science. Consequently, Einstein placed his faith in a God who could give the scientist "a sense of the ultimate and fundamental ends. To make clear these fundamental ends and valuations, and to set them fast in the emotional life of the individual, seem(ed) to (him) precisely the most important function which religion has to perform in the social life of men."[129] Such ends "came into being not through demonstration but through revelation, through the medium of powerful personalities. One must not attempt to justify them, but rather to sense their nature simply and clearly."[245] These references to both revelation and personalities provide further evidence of Einstein's opposition to the ontologistic approach.

However, in spite of his candid comments on religion, Einstein could not countenance the idea of a "personal" God with the power to act in the world. In his view, the hypothesis of causality was indispensable.[246] His God is neither playing dice nor interfering with the causal order or, for that matter, the freedom of the scientist. Understandably wary of the common subjective interpretations of the "personal," Einstein was eager to escape from the "merely personal,"[112] from "the futility of human desires and aims to the sublimity and marvellous order which reveal themselves both in nature and in the world of thought."[247] In general, he was fully committed to a comprehensive emancipation of the individual from all forms of anthropomorphism.

Yet only a living God could have already made ultimate decisions which allowed the scientist to relinquish his own subjective ones. Nothing less than a superior Being could provide for the exposure of delusion and fantasy. On one occasion, Einstein spoke at some length in terms of the "superpersonal,"[248] in spite of its anthropomorphic associations. For him, the initiative lies with God who has already expressed himself in the causal order, and who, therefore, has no need to be causally efficacious in the world. While the scientist is free from theologies of fear and works, he is motivated by a cosmic religious feeling.[246] Scientists are "profoundly religious people"[174] who take the works of God extremely seriously. Einstein himself regarded the scientific enterprise as a religious attempt to retrace the lines drawn by God. In a "superpersonal" or "extrapersonal" sense, his God is the scientific way, truth and life.

Einstein's distinct view of scientific freedom involves a relation beyond the self. It presupposes a centre of freedom as external reference, a living God behind the universe who engenders a cosmic religious feeling in the scientist. This feeling is not achieved by taking thought, but only by being inspired from beyond oneself. Scientists in their freedom are trapped in a vicious circle of perpetual delusion and fantasy unless they are open through the intuitive relation. Scientific commitment arises not because individuals choose science, but because science chooses them. Indeed, the scientist lives by faith. He believes in a superior intelligence and strives to apprehend what he has already expressed in the causal order. The scientist grows in a trust and knowledge of the rationality of the universe. He responds to that rationality through the intuitive relation in order to help his unbelief. The Christian thinker can hardly miss the conceptual affinities.

It is of the very nature of modern science to identify and to advance beyond the inadequacies of existing ways of scientific thinking. Scientific wisdom involves continuing revision and reinterpretation. Refutation is only a possible logical check on commitment to an ever-expanding apprehension of the universe.[134] Without such commitment to responsive, responsible action, scientific wisdom degenerates into scientific information. Consequently, in the hands of non-scientists, the inevitable compilations are infinitely difficult to integrate. In fact, part of the business of scientists is to root out false discontinuities in their private thinking. This conceptual grooming renders them more capable of recognizing and investigating real discontinuities in the public corpus of scientific knowledge.[249] Without an adequate grasp of fundamental principles to guide them or the necessary freedom to pursue intrinsic connections, scientists are left stranded on the apparently incohesive factual surfaces of their disciplines.

Although there are discontinuities in modern science, fragmentations have no place in scientific researches. Scientists do not shatter existing unity, unless it can be surpassed. The unification of scientific theories is extremely hard to achieve. The theories of science stand on explicated ground inspiring wonder and anticipation. Even the novice captures a sense of mystery. The labour of generations of committed scientists has been co-ordinated. Throughout the centuries, scientists have started from where others have finished. Always experiencing the impressive present and viewing the past and future through it, modern scientists realize that those theories are the proximate products of a corporate human enterprise with a direction and a purpose. In this basic respect, Einstein was no exception.

A discussion of Einstein's article on "the mechanics of Newton and their influence on the development of theoretical physics,"[250] serves several purposes. It demonstrates the utter consistency of

Einstein's thinking and his invariant commitment to scientific research, even while referring to historical scientific matters. It also exposes the intuitive relation as the backbone of scientific continuity. Lastly, it illustrates the heuristic power released by another exceptionally gifted scientist with a thorough knowledge of fundamental principles.

16. THE MECHANICS OF NEWTON

For Einstein, "the mechanics of Newton and their influence on the development of theoretical physics"[250] bristled with relevance to current scientific thinking. Einstein saw Newton as a "brilliant . . . inventor of certain key methods." He acknowledged that this great scientist "had a unique command of the empirical material available in his own day." He was also greatly impressed by the Newtonian mind which "was marvellously inventive as regards detailed mathematical and physical methods of proof."[250] But Einstein singled out as most important of all, Newton's contribution of a "self-contained system of physical causality." This theoretical edifice represented some of "the deeper features of the empirical world."[251] In other words, it appealed directly to Einstein's persistent concern about "the eternal antithesis between the two inseparable components of knowledge, the empirical and the rational."[97] This "self-contained system" did not use a multiplicity of "artificial additional assumptions."[252] It was based on "the greatest possible sparsity of . . . logically independent elements (basic concepts and axioms)."[168] "Deeper features of the empirical world" had been grasped by Newton as "the most nearly possible certain (intuitive) and complete co-ordination with the totality of sense-experiences."[168] At the beginning of this essay, Einstein directed the attention of his reader away from traditionally narrow, totally explicit accounts of scientific knowledge and development.

Scientific methods and an admirable acquaintance with the empirical data played only supporting roles. By starting from non-arbitrary hypotheses Newton was able to deduce a theoretical framework which pointed the way to greater apprehension of the structured universe. Einstein's discussion accentuated Newton's heuristic activity as grounded in scientific experience. To a historian of science, this introduction to an essay written on the occasion of the two hundredth anniversary of Newton's death might appear rather strange, perhaps even superficial. Clearly, Einstein was not contributing to a history of science. He was presenting a personal scientific appraisal of Newtonian mechanics.

After baldly claiming that "the existence of a chain of physical causation"[251] was only "a bold ambition"[251] lacking "co-ordination with sense experiences"[168] in the minds of ancient Greek materialists and all philosophers before Newton, Einstein described Kepler's law as "empirical".[251] Despite his monumental labours, Kepler's three laws provide "a complete answer to the question of *how* the planets move around the sun" but "do not satisfy the demand for causal explanation."[251] They are not "self-contained." Being "logically independent," they have "no inner connection with each other."[251] Most significantly, they do not reflect "deeper features." In particular, they cannot answer the general question of *"how the state of motion of a system gives rise to that which immediately follows it in time."* This deficiency persisted because they are "integral and not differential laws."[253] Similarily, Galileo's germane discoveries of the law of inertia and the law of bodies falling freely in the gravitational field of the earth "refer to the motion as a whole."[253]

Newton's brilliance recognized that "only by considering what takes place during an infinitely short time (differential law)"[254] could a formulation be reached which applied to all motion. Of Newton's three laws of motion, the second (differential law) carried the heaviest load. It combined an invented concept of mass, a concept of force borrowed from the current science of statics, and a "double limiting process."[253] Still, "the motion was only determined by the equation of motion in cases where the force was given."[254] "A completely causal concept of motion was achieved" using Newton's "idea that the force operating on a mass was determined by the position of all masses situated at a sufficiently small distance from the mass in question."[254] Einstein emphasized that "it is the combination – Law of Motion plus Law of Attraction – which constitutes that marvellous edifice of thought which makes it possible to calculate the past and future states of a system from the state obtaining at one particular moment, in so far as the events take place under the influence of the forces of gravity alone. The logical completeness of Newton's conceptual system lay in this, that the only causes of the acceleration of the masses of a system are *these masses themselves*."[254] In view of Einstein's researches, it is hardly surprising to find him underscoring this particular feature.

The importance of Newton's achievement was not restricted to a logical basis for the science of mechanics. His system effectively "formed the program of every worker in the field of theoretical physics."[255] This is an alternative way of indicating that it related to "the deeper features of the empirical world." With a law of force extendable to a great diversity of events, his system had the powerfully heuristic quality of obvious multiple connectivity. Its openness and incompleteness invited wider applications. Basically, "All physical events were to be traced back to masses subject to Newton's laws of motion."[255] The influence of the mechanics of Newton can be traced in theories of light, heat, gases, electricity, and magnetism, and even in the wave theory of light.[255] In fact, "Newton's fundamental principles were so satisfactory from the logical point of view that the impetus to overhaul them could only spring from the demands of empirical fact."[255] Through "inveterate habits,"[256] the generations of scientists who followed Newton became progressively less aware of the weaknesses of his system. Newton himself had wrestled with those deficiencies. His scientific progeny were less ambitious. Their familiarity with the successes of Newton's system turned their attention almost exclusively to its applications.

According to Einstein, Newton represented his system "as necessarily conditioned by experience." He "introduce(d) the smallest possible number of concepts not directly referable to empirical objects."[257] That condition forced Newton to acknowledge that "observable geometrical quantities and their course in time do not completely characterize motion in its physical aspects" [the bucket experiment].[257] This intimation of the incompleteness of his system was not ignored by Newton. On the contrary, he responded with the concepts of absolute time and space. He realized that space must "possess a kind of physical reality if his laws of motion are to have any meaning."[257] "This shadowy concept"[257] was "undefined" and "underived."[168] It revealed both the greatness of Newton's scientific wisdom and the weakness of his system. Without it his theory would have been logically more acceptable. With it his system was much more meaningful.

Newton admitted that forces acting directly and instantaneously at a distance are not characteristic of the processes of everyday life. He also conceded that "his law of gravitation is not supposed to be a final explanation."[257] Besides, his theory could not account for the strange coincidence that "the weight and the inertia of a body are determined by the same quantity (its mass)."[257] Einstein saw all three defects as relating to the "naturalness" of the theory and its "inner perfection."[252] Space affected masses but was uninfluenced by them. Mysteriously, inertial and gravitational masses were equal. Gravitational interaction was strikingly atypical. As Einstein remarked, "they merely represented unsatisfied desires of the scientific mind in its struggle for a complete and uniform conceptual grasp of natural phenomena."[217] The mind on display was, of course, that of Newton. His personal commitment to the rationality of the universe had carried him to the limitations of his own scientific theory.

Characteristic of science, "Newton's mechanics prepared the way for the field theory." It provided the differential law as "the first decisive step."[258] The resulting (Maxwell's) equations became the first serious rival to Newton's theory of motion. They formalized Faraday's concept of the "field," a new kind of physical reality in addition "to the mass point and its motion."[258] They also established that electric and magnetic interactions are propagated through space at a finite speed. Inevitably, this sequence of events increased reservations about forces acting instantaneously at a distance. Developments in the theory of the electromagnetic field, particularly Hertz's experimental work and Lorentz's theoretical labours, encouraged attempts to explain the Newtonian law of motion on the basis of field theory. Thus, Maxwell's theory "led inevitably to the special theory of relativity which, since it abandoned the notion of absolute simultaneity, excluded the existence of forces acting at a distance."[258] The special theory of relativity showed the equivalence of mass and energy, the variability of mass, the speed of light as the limiting velocity, and Newton's law of motion as the limiting case of a new law of motion.[258] Einstein argued a strong case for the continuity of scientific research.

"The general theory of relativity formed the last step in the development of the program of the field-theory."[258] According to Einstein, the causal absoluteness of space, the coincidence of the equality of inertial and gravitational masses, and the independence of force laws, the three defects of the Newtonian theory, were all eliminated. "Inertia, gravitation, and the metrical behaviour of bodies and clocks were reduced to a single field quality."[258] Spanning the centuries between Newton and modern science was an "organic development of Newton's ideas." But the findings of more recent researches involving radiation, atomic spectra, radioactivity etc., indicated "a limitation of the applicability of this whole conceptual system."[259] In particular, the current interpretations of quantum theory were characterized by indeterminism and delocalization, both of which opposed relativity theory. Einstein regarded quantum theory as useful for calculations or correct predictions but incapable of providing an adequate description of reality. Basically, Einstein could not accept the assertion that the laws of nature had to be formulated in terms of probability; nor could he reconcile himself to the reinstatement of action at a distance.

Many of his fellow scientists were convinced that the law of causation had collapsed. Einstein did not agree. Instead, he looked for a solution to the contemporary dilemma in the connections between field theory and the de Broglie-Schrödinger method, their common dependence on differential equations and the latter's treatment of discrete energy states. His concluding words, therefore, challenged those scientists who would presume to decide such ponderous matters on the basis of the available evidence. Such a momentous decision would reorient the "course of Western thought, research and practice." It would transfigure modern science as determined by Newton in a manner "like no one else before or since."[250] It might even return science to some form of pre-Newtonian acausal chaos.

It would be a grave error, however, to assume that Einstein was appealing to the authority of Newton. Indeed, Einstein implicitly rejected such tactics by demanding that "every man be respected as an individual and no man idolized."[109] Einstein was pointing through the continuous development of theoretical physics to an intuitively expanding apprehension of reality. To him, what was really at risk in a premature abandonment of the law of causation was the "whole conceptual edifice" of modern science. This edifice included corporate non-articulate scientific experience. In the Einsteinian analysis, Newton had a "greater importance than his genius warrants because destiny placed him at a turning point in the history of the human intellect."[251] Science chooses the scientist.

Einstein's urgent intention was to discourage current tendencies to reject "the modern physicist's demand for causality."[253] He served it by indicating how the law of causation and the differential law had provided the ultimate bases of all natural science from the time of Newton to the rise of modern quantum theory. Einstein was fully committed to causality. For example, in the special theory of relativity space and time are distinguished on the basis of causality. Time-like intervals represent causally related events. They are time-like intervals in all frames of reference. Likewise, space-like intervals represent non-causal events. They are space-like intervals in all frames of reference. In other words, causally related events are temporally related, whereas non-causally related events are spatially related. Consequently, simultaneity is only relevant to the former. Einstein's conceptual key, the constancy of the velocity of light, closed the door on the observation of causally independent events. Only measurements of causally past events of the world are obtainable. His own researches made him acutely aware, therefore, that causality could not be "observed." Nevertheless, they convinced him that causality was indispensable.

Einstein communicated those beliefs to Born, "I am well aware that no causality exists in relation to the observable; I consider this realization to be conclusive. But in my opinion one should not conclude from this that the *theory*, too, has to be based on fundamental laws of statistics."[260] This quotation refers to quantum theory. It is based on the intuitive relation. With no logical bridge between concepts and sense impressions, causality expresses itself in scientific theory. Consequently, Einstein refused to accept the indeterminism of quantum theory. " . . . I should not want to be forced into abandoning strict causality without defending it more strongly than I have so far. I find the idea quite intolerable that an electron exposed to radiation should choose of *its own free will,* not only its moment to jump off, but also its direction."[261] Clearly, Einstein saw in the indeterminism of quantum theory a threat to the determinate causality of relativity theory and, indeed, the ultimate basis of modern science. The scientist should have greater freedom than the electron.

In this essay, the referenced contacts with his epistemological utterances are too numerous to be ignored. The dominant theme of causality is closely associated with representations of "the deeper features of the empirical world." Even Newton is given second place after the intuitive relation because scientists are created and re-created through involvement in science. The inescapable conclusion is, therefore, that Einstein's scientific thinking forced him to address scientific questions about current scientific thinking. He tackled a contemporary scientific issue with a modern reappraisal of the achievement of Newton. He appealed to its continuous relevance as he saw it unfolded through the intervening centuries. In fact, Einstein seems to have pursued similar aims in many of his essays. A common theme appears to be the emancipation of scientific creativity from all kinds of pseudo-authority. According to Einstein, the historical details of Newton's synthesis, or even the breakthrough itself, is not as vital to science as its inexhaustible and inextinguishable light. Newton's system has enlightened scientific thinking throughout the subsequent development of theoretical physics.

Einstein was interested in the fuller significance of the mechanics of Newton. It transcended mere historicity. On another occasion, he explained how a scientist approaches his discipline. "The way in which he regards its past and present may depend too much on what he hopes for the future and aims at in the present; but that is the inevitable fate of anybody who has occupied himself intensively with a world of ideas."[244] In addition to historical background, a scientific perspective always includes an heuristic horizon. Private scientific apprehension is invariably an incomplete expression of an attempt to handle personal reactions to a reality which is only gradually accessible. To "deeply underscore the role played in the process (of scientific development) by the older theory's occasional failure to meet challenges posed by logic, experiment or observation"[262] was not Einstein's urgent concern. What was at stake was the law of causation, and with it the intuitive relation, scientific continuity and learning. Einstein demanded a stay of execution to give science time to commute the death sentence to hard labour for scientific life.

17. SUBVERSIVE SUPERFICIALITY

In general terms, Einstein believed that a scientific theory, particularly one with qualities like those of Newton's mechanics, has the power to reach across the subsequent development of modern science with a message. It addresses contemporary scientific issues at a level deeper than its articulated content. Einstein was referring, of course, to the co-existence of non-eternal scientific theories and the invariant laws of nature. The unity of the natural order exists amidst a variety of scientific theories. The rationality of the universe from which the intuitions of scientists come is contemporary with every scientific period. The laws of nature are already invariant as scientists search for a fuller apprehension of them.

Scientific experience, therefore, is required to relate effectively to that invariance. Consequently, Einstein dismissed the notion of a rigid separation of the history and interpretation of science. In his view, such things as the history of Newton's mechanics were not discoverable by so-called unbiased historical inquiry.

Basically, Einstein assumed that scientists are able to discover and to accept the inadequacies of scientific achievements like the Newtonian system, to see beyond their structures, and to trace the processes of transformation begun by their originators. According to Einstein, Newton's edifice, for example, not only initiated new kinds of scientific inquiry, it perpetually outlines their basic characteristics and inspires their development. Nevertheless, it is always possible to adhere to a scientific theory in such a manner as to ignore or to miss the promptings of the intuitive relation which can guide scientists along the way of deepening apprehension. It is also tempting to cling to particular aspects of the corpus of scientific knowledge so as to exclude or to reject the larger context in which those aspects are a part. However, scientists are "called" to serve in the temple of science, to grow up into a fuller and fuller understanding of the universe. In general, therefore, the intuitive relation disturbs their scientific complacency and enables them to resist the onslaught of failure. Scientists are liberated from fear and hesitancy into trust and hope. They realize scientific freedom and creativity mingled with a humble dependence on the natural order.

Einstein believed that, like Newton, scientists can relate to present scientific theories from beyond them, for the rationality of the universe inspires them so to speak. In a profound sense, Newton and that ilk are pioneers to every scientific period, not just their own. There is always the intuitive relation which must not be forgotten. The scientific enterprise is not merely a series of generations of scientists each encased on its own theoretical and experimental setting. It is rather a scientific community of experience stretching across those generations so that the theories which it discovers can evoke the scientific past in a way which strikes a chord in the experience of the scientific present. It is not simply a question of logical rules of the past and present. As Einstein demonstrated, past scientific achievements can still enlighten scientists as individual researchers with particular insights.

By the presence and impact of the intuitive relation the corpus of scientific knowledge transmits with power, is received with power and justifies itself wherever science advances. It conveys apprehension about the universal significance of science. The continuing influence of scientific researches gives resilience to the faith and hope of scientists. Their feeble rationality cannot cope with the rationality of the universe. However, the rationality of the universe comes to them in the form of the intuitive relation, and scientists are justified by faith. Ever conscious that they fall far short of comprehension, scientists are guardians of a delicate unity of humility and assertion. That frail unity proclaims not the merits of a scientific system, but the rationality of the universe to which all science points.

From an Einsteinian perspective, the claim that the four Gospels address contemporary issues of Christian living seems inoffensive to reason. When coupled with the assertion that the various Gospels present aspects of the Word of God who is the same yesterday and today and for ever (Heb. 13 v. 3), it has a vaguely familiar ring. If it is also associated with the proclamation that there is one Lord, Jesus Christ, through whom all things are and through whom we exist (Cor. 8 v. 6), then interested scientists are immediately carried beyond mere curiosity to the realms of formal analogy. They anticipate that the counterpart of scientific experience, Christian living, is required in order to relate authentically to Jesus Christ. Consequently, they assume that the historical and interpretative elements of the biblical record of Jesus Christ are inseparable and, therefore, the historical Jesus can never be detected by impersonal, abstract and arbitrary literary techniques.

Reasoning by analogy does not, of course, guarantee apprehension. But when an extensive correspondence is so far from exhaustion, it is necessary to look carefully at both enterprises, in case the pursuit of one could formally enrich the pursuance of the other. In fact, few Christian thinkers could read the last few paragraphs without wondering whether the author had not adapted elements of theological thinking to cope with the complexity of modern science. The discussion of the origins of Einstein's views on scientific thinking presented later in this essay will dispel such suspicions. Meanwhile, it is simply observed that Einstein's aversion to *ad hoc* methods was hardly conducive to deliberate adaptations.

To get back on the rails, the role of the intuitive relation appears once again as a pale reflection of the ministry of the Holy Spirit, and the rationality of the universe sounds like a faint echo of the Word of God. The sequential discoveries of scientific theories are formally similar to the progressive revelations of the biblical approaches to

topics like the problem of suffering. Apparently, modern science
has its major prophets including Kepler, Galileo and Newton, but
one rational unity, while Christianity has the Apostles, but one
Lord. Complacency in both science and theology stultifies all
understanding but its own. The scientific community of experience
resembles in several respects the Church Universal. Both transcend
cultural and temporal differences. Their members live in hope, are
justified by faith, and are known by the fruits of their labours.
Perhaps there is more than formal analogy involved. A full investigation is required. In any case, it is apparent that scientific and
theological thinking are not necessarily diametrically opposed.

Obviously scientists of an Einsteinian persuasion find it particularly difficult to communicate with Christians who have selected
information from philosophies and histories of science and modern
science. Using non-scientific criteria, non-scientists tend to pluck
ideas from those sources to support preconceived notions of scientific method. Scientists cannot accept such exercises as legitimate
attempts to do justice to scientific research and thinking.[263] For all
most scientists know, those concoctions may be acceptable
approaches to an ecclesiastical history of ideas. What practising
scientists have learned, sometimes at great cost, is that reasons
which sound good are not the same as good sound reasons. For
them, acceptance of such descriptions of the development of scientific research is tantamount to a rejection of science. Basically, they
deny all that Einstein defended.

In any case, many Christians reap what they sow. Their fragile
systems cannot survive contact with the concrete contents of
modern scientific research. Sooner or later, they run up against the
boundaries set up by their arbitrary constructions. When this
happens, they become confused or enslaved by their inventions
because they lack scientific wisdom. However, they will not be
denied conclusions. The sooner they hit inconsistencies, the more
chance they have of concluding that modern science is anarchic or
that scientists don't really know what they are doing half of the
time. In exceptional cases, theologians even attempt to convince
their students of the intellectual bankruptcy of scientists and technologists. Their comments on science and technology sometimes
even include contextually denuded quotations of eminent persons.
For example, the theoretician John Robert Oppenheimer once said,
"Scientific discussion is explaining to each other what we don't
know."[264] Or the technologist Werner von Braun stated that "Basic

research is what I am doing when I don't know what I am doing."[265] Those remarks presuppose a sound working knowledge of scientific research. When isolated, they become easy targets for the humourless arbitrary logic of theological extremists. Fortunately, more enlightened scholarship seems to prevail. However, arbitrary constructions cannot in general protect and promote the freedom of thought. They are incapable of respecting new knowledge by which interdisciplinary exchange is accelerated.

The later Christians meet self-imposed limitations, the less likelihood there is that they will recognize what arbitrary conceptual devices are and what damage they can do. Consequently, they are ill-prepared for the discovery that science and scientists can only be appreciated through an openness to the instructive, regulative and conservative roles of scientific learning. They are in no position to agree with Einstein that scientific learning supplies the "hygiene in the sphere of the mind."[266]

The Christian's need of scientific learning was probably never more urgent. The growth of scientific knowledge in the various natural sciences is so rapid that it is impossible for one person to embrace it. Increasing specialization makes any attempt to integrate scientific information appear foolish. An apparently more manageable, but actually no less ambitious enterprise, is the formal unity of scientific knowledge. It appeals to many Christians because it confines attention to form, i.e., to an analysis of conceptual devices and experimental procedures (methodology). Also, results, discoveries, theoretical details and case studies, in short the concrete contents of science, can be regarded as ripe for the illustrative picking. In this view, they merely serve the so-called universality of the scientific method or methods and remote discussions of induction, definition, hypotheses, falsification etc. An almost exclusive methodological emphasis re-orients interest from the empirical grounding of scientific concepts toward self-defeating arbitrary constructions. According to Einstein, scientific knowledge and experience must be combined in order to make contact with reality.

Repeated reference has been made to the years of "labour and activity" of individual scientists. Those years have more than their fair share of unsuccessful attempts to construct acceptable theories, to explain anomalous effects, to synthesise new compounds, to design novel experiments, and to observe unfamiliar phenomena. Yet scientists struggle on and seldom report negative results. All this work is not entirely lost to science. The success of one theory often annihilates the tenability of several others. The synthesis of a new family of compounds increases the chemist's knowledge of molecular structure. Frequently, the reported method of synthesis conveys a great deal of information to experimentalists. Implicitly, it can prohibit useless repetition of unpublished unsuccessful procedures. In a nutshell, scientific achievements communicate to scientists much about the feasibility of alternative approaches to particular problems. On occasions, they also rely on a knowledge of past unpublishable scientific failures. "To be sure, it is not the fruits of scientific research that elevate a man and enrich his nature, but the urge to understand, the intellectual work, creative or receptive. Thus, it would surely be inappropriate to judge the value of the Talmud by its intellectual fruits."[172]

Non-scientists cannot hope to read those signs properly, even if they suspect their existence. Consequently, as they attempt to integrate scientific information, there is always the likelihood that they will reintroduce errors already disposed of along the arduous course of scientific development. To borrow freely more of Brown's words, Christians are strongly advised to find out from scientific sources what they are going to talk or write about. This will make it a good deal more likely that they will present and publish credible comments and reviews.[267] Thinking scientifically is a matter of judging on the basis of all kinds of scientific knowledge and experience. Without the acquaintance and guidance of the latter the probability of increasing scientific apprehension is drastically reduced. Indeed, there is abundant evidence to show that Christians who are very poorly read in science rarely make valid pronouncements on scientific subjects.

This state of affairs may not unduly perturb those Christians who continue to erect prefabricated edifices using culled scientific ideas. It is subversive as far as science is concerned. Holton made this abundantly clear. "The detailed study of the historical situation is, to my mind, an important first step in those discussions which try to base epistemological considerations on 'real' cases. This is not always done easily; but it is through the examination of historically valid cases that we can best become aware of the preconceptions which underlie all philosophical study."[268] A brief look at Einstein's four papers supports Holton's views.

If students of the natural sciences listen to, or read, contrived accounts of "scientific method," they have a reasonable chance of recognizing discrepancies, omissions and incongruities. Still, if

Einstein is correct, even they will encounter considerable difficulties. "Only those who realize the immense efforts and, above all, the devotion without which pioneer work in theoretical science cannot be achieved are able to grasp the strength of the emotion out of which alone such work, remote as it is from the immediate realities of life, can issue."[246] Non-scientists, on the other hand, have almost no hope of exposing prefabrication. They are more liable to be impressed by authorative poses than by authentic detailed case studies. Thus, they are confined to superficial connections bounded by the tenets of some philosophical, historical, or theological contrivance. In other words, too many Christians are content with tacit dogmatism. The latter is, of course, anathema to the freedom of scientific thought. It is also contemptuous of the regulative, instructive and conservative roles of scientific learning. It is small wonder that many of the clergy are heard loudly decrying the triumphalist militancy of science. After all, they are attacking an arbitrary product of their own imaginations.

Philosophers and historians of science have disciplines in their own right. If Christians are wise enough to familiarize themselves and others with the rudiments of those subjects, who are scientists to interfere? In this regard scientists are laymen. But they are entitled to expect authentic representation of their subject. In its absence, they will suspect Christians' understanding of both philosophies and histories of science. This fundamental inadequacy does not, of course, prove an incompetent grasp of philosophies and histories of science. But, when a proposed analysis of science is so far from examining its primary material, it is necessary to look closely at the arguments presented.

No one can possibly provide a valid presentation of science unless he first distinguishes modern science from philosophies and histories of science. In deference to all three disciplines, and therefore to theology itself, Christians should recognize, spell out and respect the disciplinary differences. The alternative is to maintain a prudent silence where apprehension fails and until homework is done. However, the part of a passive spectator is unworthy of the Christian. As the course of events has already shown, it is bound to result in cultural disaster or ostracism. Christians should realize that, if their teachings ignore or isolate the great scientific corpus and its dynamics, their words, however eloquent and elegant, will probably receive the same treatment from many scientific researchers. Christians should, therefore, encourage those with scientific experience to participate in theological dialogue. This will counteract to some extent the damage done by others who dogmatically dismiss such contributions as irrelevant even on scientific matters.

To depend exclusively on philosophies and histories of science appears strange, if not perverse, to working scientists. Those subjects rely ultimately on private and public scientific accounts of researches. Without first-hand experience of research, many philosophers and historians of science reinterpret, refashion and recontextualize what practising scientists have said or reported. They risk false integrations and premature systematizations of scientific information. One need search no further than the theories of relativity for examples of scientific knowledge which have been appealed to as supporting numerous diverse extra-scientific studies. Christians interested in modern science and scientific thinking should take the bull by the horns. They should relate as directly as possible to scientific research.

One way of achieving this is to pursue enthusiastically committed Christians who have attained distinction *within* their scientific disciplines. The humble activity of listening to them as they talk of other forms of knowledge, scholarship and service will not be pointless. Currently many scientists relate in this manner to Christian theology. What can possibly exempt professors of Old and New Testament studies, practical theology, the philosophy of religion, ecclesiastical history and systematic theology from similar roles? Or are many of them only prepared to pay lip-service to apprehension and reconciliation? The road to chaos has long been paved with lip-service to unworkable and unworked ideas. Bluntly, if Christians impose directly or indirectly an arbitrary logic of contriving on scientific information, they can only end up with some bizarre form of mythology.

Of course, Christians are free to pursue their creations for subjective aims. But they have no excuse for subjecting unsuspecting persons to their speculative devices. To project publicly false images of science is to engage in a form of cultural sabotage. As Einstein stated well over sixty years ago, "Nobody who devotes himself to science from other reasons than superficial ones, like ambition, money making , or the pleasure of brain-sport, can neglect the questions, what are the aims of science, how far are its general results true, what is essential and what based on accidental features of the development?"[269] As more Christians begin to talk and write about science responsibly, distinguishing it from technology and philosophies and histories of science, they will inevitably strengthen opposition to subversive superficiality. In the meantime, too many of them relate to science and scientists in estranged pragmatic terms. Indifferently, they talk of social responsibility, are unable to recognize legitimate technology, and remain answerable for alienating mythological modes of thought in theology and mission. Rudolf Bultmann's defense of his programme of demythologizing displays all of those characteristics. However, a discussion of scientific, technological and everyday thinking prepares the way for a brief consideration of Bultmann's views of modern scientific thinking.

18. SCIENTIFIC, TECHNOLOGICAL AND EVERYDAY THINKING

If scientific thinking is so special, why did Einstein claim "that the whole of science is nothing more than a refinement of everyday thinking?"[270] Without any specialized training, the average citizen gathers an enormous amount of reliable information about people, events, and objects within his environment. Herbal cures, proverbs, rules of thumb, and skilled crafts have been handed down through countless generations of cultures throughout the world. Many of them have survived both the rise and progress of modern science, whereas much superstition and ignorance have been eliminated. Clearly, there are vast resources of information more astonishing than scientific knowledge. Indeed, modern science draws unrefined material from them as it expands human propensities for apprehending, relating to and living in the world. Polanyi clothed the bare affinities sketched by Einstein. "The solution of riddles, the invention of practical devices, the recognition of indistinct shapes, the diagnosis of an illness, the identification of a rare species, and many other forms of guessing right seem to conform to the same pattern" as that of "the recovery of a lost recollection" and "discovery in natural sciences."[271]

With such an immense wealth of diverse information so readily available, the average citizen does not need to keep abreast of scientific progress. The relentless flow of new material from modern science convinces him that such a task is impossible anyway. Consequently, cultural affinities and technological prowess conspire to convince non-scientists, including many theologians, that they can evaluate the scientific enterprise on the basis of its practical results. Thus, as Einstein explained, they arrive at a completely false conception of science. Inevitably, they confuse science and technology and, therefore, the progress of science and the development of technology.

According to Einstein, common-sense conceptual systems are constructive and speculative.[272] They too are based on both experience and intuition. Their greater logical disunity makes them more vulnerable than scientific theories to the same forms of criticism. Yet the validity of common-sense systems is largely taken for granted by most people until a problem raises doubts. As long as those systems work satisfactorily, doubts about them are usually suspended. Distinctively, science in its search for greater logical unity wrestles with doubts for fundamentally different ways of perceiving the world. It attempts to bring them to the microscope, to identify them and to learn from them. Scientists achieve this through openness to the rationality of the universe. By exercising freedom of inquiry but subordinating intuitive and critical faculties to the natural order, scientists glimpse new horizons. Contrary to popular opinion, those activities are not the preserve of the privileged. They are not confined to scientific genius. All scientific researchers practise them in varying combinations. Even Niels Bohr agreed with Einstein about basic features. "The task of science is both to extend the range of our experience and to reduce it to order . . . As our knowledge becomes wider, we must always be prepared, therefore, to expect alterations in the points of view best suited for the ordering of our experience."[273]

Bondi is convinced that "much deep physics may be hidden, not in the basic structure of our minds, but in what entered and formed our minds at an early age in a rather simple way"[274] Behind his repeated references to the amount of physics tacitly learned in the first few years of childhood lies the realization that much of what a person learns as a child he continues to believe as an adult. Amazingly, children accommodate an enormous influx of information as common sense, whereas adults absorb the same material only after intense intellectual effort. Bondi also claimed that "a good deal of the high-grade physics, derived normally from rather refined observations, is already inherent in what is common knowledge."[274] However, as a child grows he learns from others how to speak of the things around him and how to relate to them. He conforms by using the conceptual constructions of parents, peers and pedagogues.[275]

There are, of course, exceptions. Einstein offered an interesting explanation of his great success in science. "I sometimes ask myself," he admitted frankly, "how did it come that I was the one to develop the theory of relativity? The reason, I think, is that a normal adult never stops to think about problems of space and time. These are things which he has thought of as a child. But my intellectual development was retarded, as a result of which I began to wonder about space and time only when I had already grown up. Naturally, I could go deeper into the problem than a child with normal abilities."[276]

Einstein recognized that the societally limited critical abilities of children tend to confine their attention to imitation, repetition and acquisition, often at the expense of creative play and investigation. To a great extent, the individual acquires conceptual systems from elders. This process occurs either overtly by education or covertly by societal contacts. "The greater part of our knowledge and beliefs has been communicated to us by other people through the medium of a language which others have created."[277] It seems that most of the things that a child believes are necessary to a satisfactory performance in life. Later in life, the vast majority of people find it difficult, if not impossible, to recall their original reasons for believing them.[275]

The more a person relies on the primitive concepts of everyday life "the more difficult it becomes amidst the mass of inveterate habits to recognize the concept as an independent creation of thinking."[256] In fact, few people can persuade others of the validity of their beliefs. They have taken most of them for granted for so long. Besides, the very foundations of those beliefs have probably moved with the general growth and processing of scientific information.[27] In other words, the advance of science has slowly, almost imperceptibly, shifted the various equilibria in the overall system of cultural values.[3]

This diffusion of information cuts the beliefs of many people adrift.[278] The decreased logical unity requires a conceptual readjustment. There are, however, inertial factors. Progressively, the concepts used to describe the constraints imposed upon a person by the social and natural world become more strongly infused with his own values, interests and perspectives. Satisfaction with previous performances waxes with age. The spirit of inquiry wanes with increasing responsibilities. They conspire to widen the gap between apprehension and information, and to entrench outmoded systems of thought.

The difference between apprehension and information in the hands of the young and old is neatly captured in a story told of the young Max Planck. Not long after he had arrived in Berlin, Planck stopped at the entrance office to the university. He asked the elderly man in charge, "Please tell me in which room does Professor Planck lecture today?" The old man patted the forgetful Planck on the shoulder as he advised, "don't go there, young fellow. You are much too young to understand the lectures of our learned Professor Planck."[279] Eventually, established ways of thinking become so deep-seated that they close the individual off from reality. It requires deliberate and sustained effort to keep this particular wolf from the door. In one way or another, everyone behaves as a pragmatist at some time or another. Scientists do, for example, when they apply, but refuse to assimilate, a new theory.

Einstein believed that "scientific concepts begin with those used in ordinary language for the affairs of everyday life, but they develop quite differently. They are transformed and lose the ambiguity associated with them in ordinary language, gaining in rigor so that they may be applied to scientific thought."[280] He cited the vector as a simple illustration. Polanyi agreed with Einstein's description of the nature and origins of scientific concepts, "Natural science deals with facts borrowed largely from common experience. The methods by which we establish facts in everyday life are therefore logically anterior to the special premisses of science and should be included in a full statement of these premisses."[281] Scientific concepts and propositions are founded on measurements lending themselves to mathematical formulation.[282] The progress of science depends on the expanding expression of the sum total of its knowledge. Like the terms of a geometric series, science spans sequentially greater domains within the natural order. In the process, it is transformed by the inclusion of higher terms. The unification of scientific theories is a response to the unity of the universe. Science expresses itself most effectively, but always incompletely, in mathematical terms. In doing so, it depends on a continuing refinement of the ancient inventions of language, writing and counting.

Actually, that "things" are "as they are perceived by us through our senses" is an illusion that "dominates the daily life of man and animals(.That) is also the point of departure in all of the sciences, especially of the natural sciences."[283] The visible spectrum forms only a small band within the vast range of electromagnetic radiation. The mechanics of terrestial bodies involves velocities small compared with the speeds of galaxies and light. The global fluctuations of temperature and pressure are extremely narrow relative to those of stellar events. Audible tones represent "a small province in the world of inaudible vibrations."[284]

Einstein's theme of refinement is clearly apposite. The explanatory power of scientific theory is required to apprehend those natural orders. Creativity and mathematical rigour carry scientists beyond the immediate limitations of the senses to the invisible and inaudible *via* the inarticulate. Scientific researchers are uniquely part of the more general pattern of cultural advancement. "Without creative personalities able to think and judge independently, the upward development of society is as unthinkable as the development of the individual personality without the nourishing soil of the community."[277]

In creating modern science humankind invented and developed ways of thinking how to relate complex phenomena which go far beyond direct experience. Certainly, no one could have known in advance how far-reaching those ways would be. Nor can anyone predict their future relevance. However, for most thinkers the present theories of biology, chemistry, mathematics, physics and the other sciences represent an achievement whose magnitude and intensity are both surprising and impressive. It would be perverse to deny modern science its achievements simply because they have been exploited by those seeking wealth or power for their selfish interests, instead of being used for the general benefit of humankind.

Human sensory equipment is limited. Nevertheless, with the combination of intuition and reason, scientists have managed to apprehend multifarious aspects of reality. They range from subnuclear processes through mechanisms of neutral transmission and chemical reactions of inheritance (the genetic code) to life-histories of stars and galaxies. With sound reasons for assuming that the laws of physics and chemistry are the same throughout the universe, scientists estimate the age of the universe, its present size and the total numbers of galaxies, stars and atoms.[285] Einstein spoke for many scientists when he expressed his unfading wonder that scientific thought finds order to exist among the apparently disparate phenomena of nature. "It is a fact that the totality of sense experiences is so constituted as to permit putting them in order by means of thinking – a fact which can only leave us astonished, but which we shall never comprehend. One can say: the eternally incomprehensible thing about the world is its comprehensibility."[286]

In order to be able to understand scientific thinking, Christians must first come to terms with how scientists cope with the "eternally incomprehensible thing about the world." Every scientist knows that scientific research alters his perception of the world. On the pedestrian level, hexagonal structures encountered in everyday life remind organic chemists of aromatic compounds. Wall-paper designs trigger the crystallographer's knowledge of two-dimensional space groups. A jet flying across the clear blue sky recalls the tracking of an elementary particle in a cloud-chamber.[287] Scientists change with their apprehensions of the natural order, whereas technologists adapt the natural order to meet their immediate requirements. Both are, of course, committed to unknown unforeseen consequences which will probably dictate long-term changes. The vital distinction, drawn by Einstein, is that scientific change is discovered, unlike technological change which is made.

The prime example of the unintended consequences of modern technological development is the cultural impact of the automobile. It has changed community living, eating and work habits, recreational outlets, sexual behaviour, transportation networks, trading patterns, governmental taxation, national foreign policies and international commerce. The natural environment, the social structure and the physical condition of the individual have been influenced beyond all expectations of those who produced the first generation of automobiles. As already indicated, the twentieth century faces an irreversible, unfathomable disruption of deeply instilled cultural modes caused by the profusive gadgetry of commercially enslaved technological innovation.

Many years ago, Einstein wrote, "Science cannot create ends and, even less, instill them in human beings; science, at most, can supply the means by which to attain certain ends."[288] Currently, society legislates for profiteering in genetic engineering, while committed scientists consolidate their pioneering. The legitimate way to deal with "the comprehensibility of the world" is to experience a growing sympathy with it. This can be achieved only in so far as scientists are prepared to trust and obey its orders. Of course, scientists can abandon their vocation at any time. The freedon of science depends on the personal freedom of the scientist who can defect without recrimination. By patenting their discoveries scientists can deny their debts to scientific predecessors and contemporaries. But they cannot have their cake and eat it. Science is answerable only for the discoveries. It has nothing to do with the making of commercial processes, products or profits. Personal commitment to science precludes ulterior enterprises. Science never strays from the fold. It is the fold from which the wealth-wolf snatches a few scientists.

As already indicated, the personal commitment of the scientist does not eliminate scientific objectivity. On the contrary, scientific researchers submit their theories to objective reality, the rationality of the universe. Nevertheless, objective reality is apprehended by empirically-loaded theories and theory-laden observations and experiments. In other words, there is no neutral foundation beyond the rationality of the universe. Scientists are wholly committed to increasing humankind's apprehension of the natural order. In fact, this commitment derives from the pre-established harmony between thought and reality. It transcends the limited apprehensions of individual scientists and their reliance on objectivity. It is pre-reflective and perficient. Like a "little piece of nature"[289] the scientist changes when the realms of science are expanded. Strictly impersonal knowledge cannot exist. On the other hand, scientific knowledge is not "merely personal" or subjective. It is personal in the sense that it is guided only by the rational requirements of reality.

Einstein's dynamic conception of knowledge is utterly dependent on his postulate of the fundamental intuitiveness of knowledge. Scientists are always intimately involved in the scientific enterprise and, therefore, in scientific thinking. They are constrained by the greater unobservable rationality as it intimates itself in the lesser observable phenomena. Scientists travel along personal hysteresis loops, experiencing an ever-expanding apprehension of the natural order. Scientific theories are rational because they expose and explain intelligible dynamic structures in nature. In short, they contact reality.

Incontrovertibly, science makes possible the contriving of things that improve or devalue life. But it is not unique in this respect. As already noted, science does not deal with societal issues. It neither dictates nor recommends technological transformations of possibilities into actualities. It leaves such matters to society and technology to decide and to harness, respectively. A succinct description of technology was provided by Polanyi. "Technology comprises all acknowledged operational principles and endorses the purposes which they serve."[290] In contradistinction, scientists guard jealously the freedom of research and the conservative, regulative and instructive roles of scientific learning. The "delicate little plant of curiosity of inquiry stands mainly in need of freedom."[92] Of course, its fruits are always inspected and given the stamp of public scientific approval before they appear on the market of ideas. Without this "inner freedom," scientists cannot remain open to the rationality of the universe. Its loss places scientific commitment in jeopardy. Besides, when denied access to the free exchange of scientific knowledge within the scientific community, scientists are more severely exposed to the dangers of fantasies and delusions. The notion of patenting scientific discoveries is, therefore, intrinsically non-scientific.

To the vast majority of non-scientists talk of scientific freedom seems too remote, if not irrelevant. They are inclined, therefore, to confuse scientific progress with technological development. In Scotland, the study of physics retains its old name of natural philosophy as a salutory reminder that science is a search for an understanding of nature, not a striving for power over it.[291] Contemporary science does not promise a comprehensive explanation of the universe. It is too aware of the incompleteness and uncertainty of its theories to claim mastery of nature. To confer extraneous authority on science is just another way of depriving it of its freedom. According to Einstein, the universe alone, or more precisely the God who reveals himself in it, has the authority to grant scientists the freedom to choose to believe, to inquire or even to defect.

Information promises power. Who would deny that the scientific knowledge gained over the past sixteen decades or so has been matched by immense technological development? The most senior of our citizens knew in childhood the horse as the only alternative to the steam engine.[291, 292] The candle or oil-lamp was their standard form of domestic illumination. Gas-light was a splendid improvement, electric light a rare luxury. The journey to the moon was listed under science fiction. The physicist A. M. Taylor hit the nail on the head when he said, "This transformation of our civilization has come so swiftly that our thinking is distorted."[291] Decades earlier, Einstein had predicted that "the morbid symptoms of present-day society" will be explained by future historians "as the childhood ailments of an aspiring humanity, due entirely to an excessive speed at which civilization was advancing."[12] Since before the turn of the century, the rates of scientific progress and technological development have made it extremely difficult for non-scientists to avoid confusing them. However, Einstein the optimist believed that contemporary societal troubles are only the prelude to a greater material well-being.

Nevertheless to dismiss scientific research as a means of enhancing the "possibility that man may at last be freed from the burden of physical toil"[281] is to misunderstand the whole scientific endeavour. Science does not issue permits for the technical control of nature. Even a cursory investigation of Werner Heisenberg's uncertainty principle is sufficient to show that. Prediction has limited application in science. Attempts to extend its range to large scale manipulations of nature do not appeal to scientists. The belated emergences of organo-metallic, fluorocarbon and metallic cluster chemistry are further striking examples of the limitations of prediction in the natural sciences. Failure and ignorance are constant companions in scientific research. They are permanent reminders of the subtlety of nature and the futility of hidden agendas for its exploitation or control. The unpredictability of science is beyond question. Most scientists, like Einstein, have found that "being where the future was being brewed"[293] is difficult enough to handle without the additional restrictions of ulterior motives.

"Those whose acquaintance with scientific reseach is derived chiefly from its practical results easily develop a completely false notion of the mentality of men who, surrounded by a skeptical world, have shown the way to kindred spirits scattered wide through the world and the centuries. Only one who has devoted his life to similar ends can have a vivid realization of what has inspired these men and given them the strength to remain true to their purpose in spite of countless failures."[247] Even fresh graduates of science have considerable difficulty in identifying properly with Einstein's remarks. This should come as no surprise to the clergy. It is common knowledge that raw graduates of divinity rarely lecture convincingly on matters relevant to life in the parish until they have personally experienced that enriching vocation.

In the absence of personal scientific experience, the plethora of biological, chemical, electrical, mechanical and atomic applications encourages the popular imagination to equate technological devices and feats with scientific achievements. Consequently, the motives behind the beating out of swords or plough-shares and the reasons for constructing nuclear bombs or reactors are frequently identified as those which led to the discovery of malleable ore and nuclear energy. Besides, by interpreting the experimental nature of science as the vehicle of its instrumental aim, many non-scientists argue that technology is implicit in the predictive aspirations of science. In this view, a scientific experiment can be described as 'breaking and entering' the natural world. Denied the key to nature, scientists pick the lock, smash a window or kick down the door. As far as most scientists are concerned an experiment is a question put to nature without intimidation. Of course, both the question and its answer have personal elements. The scientist's passion for apprehension is as necessary to him as the air he breathes. But, for him, the manipulation of nature is piracy on the high seas of rationality.

The felony is compounded, for example, by the powerful technological medium of television.[294] Many of its advertisements depend on tenuous references to scientific constituents or properties of products or processes. Simultaneously they exploit and reinforce the common misconceptions that scientific statements are infallible and immutable. No responsible scientist would make such claims. Nor should anyone concede them. The inability to discriminate between modern science and its commercial exploitation on the small screen predisposes many people to regard those perversions as authentic manifestations of manipulative scientific thinking. Although it is not a new problem, this particular form of misrepresentation has grown to pernicious proportions in a socially-disintegrating mass-communications-ridden age. In large measure, the mass media are restricted by vested interests and self-seeking opportunists. They have contributed greatly to the decline of conversation while gaining an excessive influence on public opinion. Most important of all, they have abused their privileges by inexorably commingling scientific fact and fiction.[295]

The twentieth century is not a scientific age. Human activity includes a great deal of scientific research, but it can hardly be described as the dominant preoccupation of humankind. Scientific apprehension is not common place. What is characteristic of modern societies is the unebbing effort to use the results of scientific researches for the whole spectrum of human purposes. In this particular pragmatic age, there is a widespread awareness of the continuous increase of technological capacity which the results of scientific research make possible. The intrinsic value of science is generally ignored or even denied with inevitable consequences. Science and technology are seen then as the twin horns of the major societal dilemma. The energy that should be used to apprehend the realities is consequently dissipated by pragmatic minds employing expedient means to achieve unjustified ends, including the extermination of unrecognizable modern scientific thinking. The story of the Tower of Babel is also the story of this so-called scientific age.

On one occasion, Holton first reminded his reader that Einstein had said, "I AM A LITTLE PIECE OF NATURE."[289] He then proposed the following general hypothesis. "There is a mutual mapping of the style of thinking and acting of the genial scientist on the one hand, and the chief unresolved problems of contemporary science on the other."[296] Christians can probably hear distant echoes of the theme of the garden of Eden. They might even be reminded of the miracle that, in the birth, life, death, resurrection and ascension of Jesus, the Word of God offered Himself as humanity's true response in person, word and activity to God the Creator. Both scientists and Christians are left stranded when they reject the respective higher rationality. Apostasy renders them unable to refine authentically everyday thinking, for their ways are no longer the ways of the universe nor of its Creator. The ways of Bultmann are now considered.

19. THE WRONG EQUATIONS

Reputedly one of the greatest scholars in the field of New Testament studies, Rudolf Bultmann, described in the Shaffer and the Cole Lectures of 1951 what is involved in "de-mythologizing." He also dealt with objections levelled at his programme. Published in 1958 as a booklet entitled *Jesus Christ and Mythology*, their contents were delivered, at least in part, at thirteen theological institutions in North America. This was fifteen years after the publication of Einstein's essay on *Physics and Reality*.

According to Bultmann, "the task of de-mythologizing received its first impulse from the conflict between the mythological views of the world contained in the bible and the modern views of the world which are influenced by scientific thinking . . ."[297] Distinctively, " . . . de-mythologizing takes the modern world-view as a criterion. To demythologize is to reject not Scripture or the Christian message as a whole, but the world-view of Scripture, which is the world-view of a past epoch . . ."[298] Bultmann's "method of interpretation of the New Testament . . . tries to recover the deeper meaning behind the mythological conceptions . . . Its aim is not to eliminate the mythological statements but to interpret them."[299] On first encounter, Bultmann's programme appears to be a reasonable enterprise. But many scientists have immediate reservations about the existence of a singular modern world-view.

Related problems become more apparent as Bultmann's references to modern science are examined closely. "But for the present purposes," Bultmann claimed, "it is enough to say that the thinking of modern man is really shaped by the scientific world-view, and that modern men need it for their daily lives."[300] Earlier, he had stated that "mythological conceptions of heaven and hell are no longer acceptable for modern man since for scientific thinking to speak of "above" and "below" in the universe has lost all meaning . . ."[301] Later he went on to say that "(the Christian) delivers up the faith in miracles to the criticism of science and in so doing validates such criticism."[302]

As scientists begin to correlate all of those statements, their common content arouses suspicion. Consistently, they claim or presuppose an influential relation between scientific thinking or a modern scientific world-view and everyday thinking or modern views of the world. Significantly, Bultmann confined himself to repeated references to causation. According to Einstein, it had remained but a "bold ambition" in the minds of the Greek materialists and all philosophers before Newton.[251] This raises important questions. Did Bultmann believe that "modern man" thinks scientifically? Or did he consider that the influence of science on the thinking of "modern man" was adequately described as an encouragement to think and view things in terms of cause and effect?

As repeatedly noted, Einstein believed that "the whole of science is nothing more than a refinement of everyday thinking."[270] He was also convinced that "scientific research can reduce superstition by encouraging people to think and view things in terms of cause and effect."[169] He did not consider, however, scientific and everyday thinking as equivalent. On the contrary, he stated clearly that scientific thinking cannot be satisfied with the lack of logical unity characteristic of everyday thinking.[100] Scientific thinking is the cultivation of everyday thinking by a persistent search for greater and greater logical unity in the scientific world picture.

Scientists think and experiment their way to a scientific description of the rainbow as an optical phenomenon. The everyday thinker accepts this information from scientists largely on trust. Without any sustained effort at conceptual integration, he relates pragmatically to this phenomenon. He can not suddenly think scientifically about rainbows. "The fact that on the basis of such [scientific] laws we are able to predict the temporal behaviour of phenomena in certain domains with great precision and certainty is deeply embedded in the consciousness of the modern man, even though he may have grasped very little of the contents of those laws."[166] Einstein was referring, of course, to the very important distinction between prediction and apprehension. Many Christians assume that, because they can relate in terms of prediction, they can communicate on scientific matters. Realistically, if there is such a thing as a contemporary world-view, it is intrinsically incoherent and intractably pragmatic.

Bultmann was correct when he claimed that modern views of the world are influenced by scientific thinking. But he appears to have misunderstood the nature of that influence. In fact, the description of mythology provided by Bultmann applies equally well to both the so-called world-view of biblical times and modern views of the world. Compare the following quotation with its supplied alternative reading. "Myths [pragmatic beliefs] speak about gods [ecology] and demons [technologies] as powers on which man knows himself to be dependent, powers whose favor he needs, powers whose wrath he fears. Myths [pragmatic beliefs] express the knowledge that man is not master of the world and of his life, that the world within which he lives is full of riddles and mysteries and that human life also is full of riddles and mysteries. Mythology [a modern view of the world] expresses a certain understanding of human existence. It believes that the world and human life have their ground and their limits in a power which is beyond all that we can calculate or control. Mythology [a modern view of the world] speaks about this power inadequately and insufficiently because it speaks about it as if it were a worldly power."[303]

For many scientists, the preceding alternative reading represents a fairly accurate description of the current state of affairs. Bultmann's selection of "the modern world-view" as a criterion is, therefore, fraught with difficulties. It seems to jumping from the frying pan into the fire. If every scientist, as well as layman, behaves as a pragmatist at some time or another, how can one ever hope to demythologize or to talk meaningfully of "*the* modern world-view?"

Curiously, the germ of the preceding criticism is contained in the following extract. "[Biblical eschatology] will not rise in its old mythological form but from the terrifying vision that modern technology, especially atomic science, may bring about the destruction of our earth through the abuse of human science and technology."[304] By referring to "atomic science" as a form of "modern technology," Bultmann is out of step with Einstein, Polanyi, Bondi, the vast majority of scientists, and a considerable number of technologists. This conferred equivalence on science and technology is not an isolated incident in Bultmann's defense of his programme. Nor is it without consequent conceptual distortions.

According to Bultmann, "the development of science and technology . . . procures the illusion that man is master over the world and his life."[305] "The scientific world-view engenders a great temptation, namely, that man strive for mastery over the world and over his own life."[306] These contentions are vaguely similar, but diametrically opposed, to Einstein's description of scientific thinking.[307] They are at odds with Bondi's defense of the role of technology in scientific progress[308] and Polanyi's views on scientific research.[309] Basically they obscure the originative difference between science and technology. Those remarks support the suspicion that Bultmann misunderstood essentially how scientific thinking influenced modern views of the world. Einstein, on the other hand, had already explained in *The Christian Register* that "science, in the immediate, produces knowledge, and, indirectly, means of action. It leads to methodical action if definite goals are set up in advance. For the function of setting up goals and passing statements of value transcends its domain."[310]

Moreover, if the choice had been left to Bultmann, Einstein's "delicate little plant" would never have seen the clear light of day. "By means of science men try to take possession of the world, but the world gets possession of men. We can see in our times to what degree technology brings with it terrible consequences."[311] Yet, " . . . faith acknowledges that the world-view given by science is a necessary means for doing our work within the world."[312] Considered separately, each of the many quotations can perhaps be explained away in some fashion or another. When viewed collectively and in the light of Bultmann's own emphasis on the need for freedom in the life of the Christian, suspicion hardens into conviction. Because he did not understand the rudiments of modern scientific thinking, Bultmann confused science and technology, and scientific and everyday thinking.

Amazingly, the very words used by Bultmann to describe the role of freedom in the life of the Christian are equally applicable to the part it plays in the working life of the scientist. "Genuine freedom is freedom from the motivation of the moment; it is freedom which withstands the clamour and pressure of momentary motivations. It is possible only when conduct is determined by a motive which transcends the present moment, that is, by law . . . This can only be a law which has its origin and reason in the beyond."[313] Contrast those statements with Bultmann's remark that "freedom of subjective arbitrariness believes itself to be master of the world through science and technology."[305]

Clearly, had Bultmann taken the scientific enterprise seriously enough, he might not have conferred equivalence on science and technology. On the contrary, he might have recognized crucial distinctions between the commitment and freedom of scientists and the motivation and logic of contriving of technologists, respectively. Had he read Einstein's available contributions, he would have learned of the decisive difference between scientific and everyday thinking. Instead, Bultmann oscillated between valid comments like "modern man always makes use of technical means which are the results of science,"[314] and invalid remarks such as "modern man acknowledges as reality only such phenomena or events as are comprehensible within the framework of the rational order of the universe."[315]

Some telling evidence of Bultmann's disregard of scientific thinking taxes the credulity of all who have had any contact with modern science or philosophies and histories of science. Bultmann believed that "the method of scientific thinking and inquiry is in principle the same today as it was at the beginning of methodical and critical science in ancient Greece."[300] Why didn't he conclude, therefore, that the method of scientific thinking and inquiry has always been, and always will be, incompatible with current world-views of the contents of the Bible? Had he done so, he might then have recognized that humankind has always had its mythologies.

Actually, Bultmann explained away the concrete connection between scientific and everyday thinking. "The science of today is no longer the same as it was in the nineteenth century, and to be sure, all the results of science are relative, and no world-view of yesterday or today or tomorrow is definitive. The main point is, however, not the concrete results of scientific research and the contents of a world-view, but the method of thinking from which the world-views follow."[315] In other words, Bultmann avoided the former conclusion, precisely because he was convinced that the unchanging ancient "scientific" modes of thought had become those of the "modern man."

According to Einstein, "we reverence ancient Greece as the cradle of Western science. Here for the first time the world witnessed the miracle of a logical system . . . – I refer to Euclid's geometry. This admirable triumph of reasoning gave the human intellect the necessary confidence in itself for its subsequent achievements . . . But before mankind could be ripe for a science which takes in the whole of reality, a second fundamental truth was needed . . . all knowledge of reality starts from experience and ends in it. Propositions arrived at by purely logical means are completely empty as regards reality. Because Galileo saw this, and particularly because he drummed it into the scientific world, he is the father of modern physics – indeed, of modern science altogether."[316] Moreover, Newtonian mechanics came later, and several more centuries had to pass before Einstein made his contributions. Once again, Bultmann betrayed his ignorance of modern science.

Bultmann gave as an example of "non-mythological terms" the statement that "the finiteness of the world and of man over against the transcendent power of God contains not only warning, but also consolation."[317] As far as most scientists are concerned, this statement has borrowed and, therefore, transmuted scientific and theological terminology. It employs scientific terms divorced from scientific content and is, therefore, consistent with Bultmann's separation of scientific methodology from scientific content. Like many other remarks of Bultmann, it militates against the possible acceptance of his claim that "in our day and generation, . . . we no longer think mythologically."[318] The course of history has not refuted mythology, only mythologies.[314]

By his own admission, Bultmann's programme stands or falls with his criterion. As has been shown, it depends on two erroneous assumptions, namely; the equivalence of the progress of science and the development of technology, and the parity of scientific and everyday thinking. Many Christians spend a great deal of time discussing this particular programme. It seems reasonable to assume that some of them have discussed it through the years with graduates of science, scientific researchers and technologists. At least a few of the latter must have been able to expose it. One can only conclude, therefore, that their relevant questions were stifled or dismissed as products of estranged or deficient modes of thought. Certainly, many modern scientists remain puzzled by the powerful influence of Bultmann's programme on contemporary Christian theology.

A past president of the British Society for the Philosophy of Science, L. L. Whyte, told the following story about Einstein and his new assistant Cornelius Lanczos. It contrasts sharply with the predicament of Bultmann and his followers. " . . . (I)n the early days of October 1928 – Einstein put before Lanczos a new type of wave equation or field equation and asked Lanczos to see if he could find a solution which should have certain properties. I will call them alpha, beta and gamma. Lanczos understood the problem perfectly, was intensely proud of being given such a task by Einstein, and went away feeling very humble and unsure. But he studied the equation and after three or four days – flash! – there came into his mind the perfect solution. It had all three properties that Einstein had asked for . . .

(W)hen he reached Einstein . . . he said, 'Yes, I have been able to find a solution'. He showed it to Einstein and he demonstrated that it had the required three properties. Einstein looked at him and said, 'Yes, very interesting, quite remarkable.' There was a short silence, and then he exclaimed, rather impatiently, 'But don't you see, I gave you the wrong equation. It was quite wrong!' There was a silence. These two highly intelligent men did not need to say anything, for they knew what . . . had happened."[320]

Unlike Einstein, Bultmann did not realize that he had given the wrong equations. Some Christians are still trying to find solutions to his particular problem. Too often, their silence on Bultmann's confused statements about science and technology precludes valid criticism. When it does, the credibility of their theological comments on science and technology plunges, like Rojansky's curve, below the legend. Interested scientists have grave doubts about the responses of Bultmann's followers to the created order and, therefore, about their repercussions upon theology and mission. In short, many scientists are reminded of the urgency with which Christians should seek a realistic understanding of modern scientific thinking.

20. SCIENTIFIC EXPERIENCE AND APPREHENSION

A comparison of Einstein's epistemological utterances and his four scientific papers of 1905 represents a limited but realistic attempt to understand the basic aspects of modern scientific thinking. A number of events associated, either directly or indirectly, with those papers have been discussed on many occasion and in diverse contexts. Their contents are not technical. On the contrary, they are particularly suitable for the present purpose. In any case, if the preceding preparatory discussion of Einstein's epistemological views and this phase of his scientific researches have proved intelligible without conceding the core of the matter, the following exposition should present few difficulties. An inkling of how his epistemological views and scientific researches inter-related throughout the working life of this exceptional scientific thinker casts some light on the origins and the strength of the motivation behind his remarkable scientific achievements.

First, Einstein opened his paper *On a Heuristic Viewpoint Concerning the Production and Transformation of Light* by contrasting the theoretical representations of mechanics and electromagnetic theory.[199] In fact, he pointed out that, at low frequencies or high temperature, Planck's results indicated the inadequacy of both theories. Clearly, Einstein had read Planck's famous paper on the theory of black-body radiation.[321] Only in the following year did he realize that Planck had introduced the notion of discrete energy levels of charged harmonic oscillators into physics. Planck had produced a mere device to facilitate further calculation.[322] Later, he referred to his innovation as "an act of desperation, for by nature I am peaceful and against dubious adventures."[323] Planck's admission was a direct acknowledgement that, on this occasion, he had spurned epistemology as he turned to intuition.

The mathematical complexity of Planck's work probably retarded recognition of its original conception of intrinsic discreteness in nature. This did not, however, totally eclipse its absorption. Einstein produced another form of quantization by treating radiation as a stream of localized particles or quanta. Apparently, Einstein had assimilated the "dominating role of the concept" of discreteness from Planck's work. He had "played freely" with this heuristic device "to a considerable degree unconsciously." Ultimately, he enmeshed it as a definite operational property of radiant energy by indicating some "measure of its survey over scientific experience."[107] This incident has all the markings of a striking example of what Einstein believed was the way scientists apprehend the natural order. In particular, the operation of pre-articulate elements of scientific thinking early in Einstein's scientific research probably influenced his epistemological views.

Second, there was the remarkable simultaneous development of statistical mechanics by two different scientists working at distant locations.[209] Three years before the appearance of his paper dealing with his statistical description of Brownian motion[208], Einstein had prepared his ground. He had completed and published his treatment of the conditions of thermal equilibrium and the Second Law of Thermodynamics in terms of probability.[324] As Born noted, Gibbs is not mentioned in Einstein's paper.[209] In the previous year Gibbs had published a thorough investigation of the same topic.[209] The similarity of the two approaches is particularly noticeable, although Einstein's work is less abstract. In his *Autobiographical Notes* Einstein reported that he had not known of the earlier investigation of Gibbs who, he admitted, had actually exhausted this subject.[197] "No logical path"[168] led Gibbs or Einstein from perceptions to theory, but "a growing sympathy with the natural order" could account for the coincidence.[111] The close parallelism certainly lends support to the view that scientists are guided by and subject to the rationality of the universe.[99] If one postulates the operation of the intuitive relation, this parallelism loses its element of surprise. On this basis, the scientific apprehension and experience of both scientists would be expected to follow roughly similar heuristic tracks. From an Einsteinian perspective, the coincidence looks less convincing but more impressive. Einstein had probably personal cause to think about things like the intuitive relation.

Third, two alternative approaches to Einstein's electrodynamics of moving bodies had already been published in the previous year. Two other scientists had started independently from different presuppositions. Einstein wrote to Carl Seelig in 1955, " . . . I knew only Lorentz's important work of 1895 – *La Théorie electromagnétique de Maxwell* and *Versuch einer Theorie der elektrischen und optischen Erscheinungen im bewegten Korpern* – but not Lorentz's later work, nor the consecutive investigations by Poincaré. In this sense my work of 1905 was independent."[228]

In a paper published in 1904 Poincaré discussed the Galilean Principle of Relativity and current developments in electromagnetic theory.[325] Like Lorentz, he suggested that no velocity can exceed that of light. Casting doubt on the need for an ether, he indicated that an entirely new theory was necessary. In another paper of 1905, Poincaré was the first to use the expression "Lorentz transformation." He also introduced the idea of an imaginary fourth component in the definition of the fundamental geometrical interval.[326] Many scientists think that Poincaré, the leading French mathematician of his time, would have produced the special theory of relativity had Einstein failed, or even dallied, in his quest.[327]

Lorentz was convinced that the Newtonian theory of motion was basically sound. He believed that its modification would resolve known anomalies. Still, he confessed near the beginning of his paper that "Poincaré has objected to the existing theory of electric and optical phenomena in moving bodies that, in order to explain Michaelson's negative result, the introduction of a new hypothesis has been required, and that the same necessity may occur each time new facts will be brought to light. Surely this course of inventing hypotheses for each new experimental result is somewhat artificial. It would be more satisfactory if it were possible to show by means of certain fundamental assumptions and without neglecting terms of one order of magnitude or another, that many electromagnetic actions were entirely independent of the motion of the system."[328]

The hopes of Lorentz and the criticisms of Poincaré were satisfied beyond all expectations by Einstein's theory. Regardless of his confession, the number of *ad hoc* hypotheses in Lorentz's paper ran into double figures.[329] With his heroic style, Holton has suitably dramatized this situation. "Lorentz's work can be seen somewhat as that of a valiant and extraordinary captain rescuing a patched ship that is being battered against the rocks of experimental results, whereas Einstein's work, far from being a direct theoretical response to unexpected experimental results, is a creative act of disenchantment with the mode of transportation itself – an escape to a rather different vehicle altogether."[329]

Einstein started from two fundamental postulates "conditioned by observed facts."[236] He avoided the use of mathematical approximations, and demonstrated the invariance of Maxwell's equation.[212] In a letter to Paul Ehrenfest in 1919 he explained, " . . . your difficulties with the development of relativity theory . . . arise simply because you want to base the innovations of 1905 on epistemological grounds (non-existence of the stagnant ether) instead of empirical grounds (equivalence of all inertial systems with respect to light)."[330] Scientific research had taught Einstein that epistemology only offered a negative logical check, whereas the natural order provided a positive intimation of the special theory of relativity. The commitment of Einstein's intuition was expressed as complete confidence in the principle of relativity. Unlike Lorentz and Poincaré, Einstein dared to build on it.[331]

Sixteen years later, in a lecture given at King's College, London, Einstein drew "attention to the fact that this theory is not speculative in origin: it owes its invention entirely to the desire to make physical theory fit observed fact as well as possible. We have here no revolutionary act but the natural continuation of a line that can be traced through centuries. The abandonment of certain notions connected with space, time and motion hitherto treated as fundamentals must not be regarded as arbitrary but only as conditioned by observed facts."[236] Significantly, there is no denial that his theory is constructive. Indeed, Einstein referred to it as inventive. The claim is rather that it is "not speculative in origin." This critical distinction was carefully stressed by Einstein who pointed out that observed facts "conditioned," as opposed to dictated, the "abandonment of notions."

In fact, Einstein believed that he was following in the footsteps of Newton whose " . . . endeavours to represent his system as necessarily conditioned by experience and to introduce the smallest possible number of concepts not directly referable to empirical objects are everywhere evident . . ."[257] Einstein saw his theory as much more than a mere *ad hoc* adaptation of Newton's theory. Nevertheless, he regarded it as a continuation of Newton's work, methods, and aspirations.[259]

"It is one of the essential features of the theory of relativity that it is at pains to work out the relations between general concepts and empirical facts more precisely. The fundamental principle here is that the justification for a physical concept lies exclusively in its clear and unambiguous relation to facts that can be experienced."[332] Einstein knew that the use of *ad hoc* or abitrary additional assumptions had previously and repeatedly proved inadequate in the search for a greater logical unity. Both Lorentz and Poincaré had expressed dissatisfaction with such expediencies. His own theory is far more impressive because of the simplicity of its premises, the diversity of phenomena which it correlates, and the range of its applicability.[143] Its "inner perfection" or "naturalness," though defying "exact formulation," became particularly apparent on comparison with Lorentz's work.[252] In short, very soon after the publication of his theory, Einstein had a dress rehearsal for his subsequent performance in defense of the special theory of relativity against the prosecuting results of Kaufmann.

Years later, Einstein remained consistent under much more favourable circumstances. He surprised one of his students, Ilse Rosenthal-Schneider, who recorded the incident. "Once when I was with Einstein in order to read with him a work that contained many objections against his theory . . . he suddenly interrupted the discussion of the book, reached for a telegram that was lying on the windowsill, and handed it to me with the words, 'Here, this will perhaps interest you.' It was Eddington's cable with the results of measurement of the eclipse expedition (1919). When I was giving expression to my joy that the results coincided with his calculations, he said quite unmoved, 'But I knew that the theory is correct'; and when I asked, what if there had been no confirmation of his predictions, he countered 'Then I would have been sorry for the dear Lord – the theory is correct'."[333] The theory referred to is, of course, his general theory of relativity.

Undoubtedly, Einstein was far more impressed by the logical unification or simplification of theoretical foundations than by corroboration of particular details. His scientific experiences had seen to that. The more he researched in science, the more convinced Einstein became of the pre-established harmony between thought and reality. The conviction impelled him to search for decades for a unified field theory.[334] Einstein was not overawed by scientific prediction. Scientific research had repeatedly shown him the value of an intuitive grasp of the significance of a theory.

Fourth, while discussing the origins of the special theory of relativity in his *Autobiographical Notes*, Einstein recalled how he hit upon a paradox at the age of sixteen, "his first insight into the problem of the nature of light."[214] "If I pursue a beam of light with velocity c (velocity of light in a vacuum), I should observe such a beam of light as a spacially oscillatory electromagnetic field at rest. However, there seems to be no such thing, whether on the basis of experience, or according to Maxwell's equation. From the very beginning it appeared to me intuitively clear that, judged from the standpoint of such an observer, everything would have to happen according to the same laws as for an observer who, relative to the earth, was at rest. For how, otherwise, should the first observer know i.e., be able to determine, that he is in a state of fast uniform motion?"[133] Light at rest is a contradiction in terms.

In adolescence, Einstein devised by "free play with concepts" a remarkable thought *(Gedanken)* experiment. It involved Maxwell's equations, the velocity of light, and the states of motion of two observers. This intuitive association of ideas represented what he called "the germ of the special theory of relativity."[214] Notably, its appeal to both theory and observation went unanswered. His resilient mind was not robbed of its youthful enthusiasm. One might say that the thought experiment remained a twinkle in his mind's eye. With continued striving the two postulates of the special theory of relativity would eventually emerge. The conception of this free creation and its subsequent period of gestation correspond vaguely to what Einstein described as the invention of, and free play with, heuristic "elements" in that phrase of "private thinking" which goes on "without the use of words" and "to a considerable degree unconsciously."[335] The similarities hint, yet again, at experiential grounds for his epistemological utterances. This particular correspondence seems even more probable in the light of Einstein's comments to the eminent psychologist, Max Wertheimer. In 1916, Einstein emphasized to him that curiosity and doubt, rather than logical clarity and scientific conviction, were characteristic of his thoughts at that time.[336]

Both as a student and in his early scientific work, Einstein was greatly influenced by David Hume and Ernst Mach. Hume's penetrating criticism of "common-sense assumptions and dogmas"[337] had a lasting effect on Einstein. It is reflected, for instance, in Einstein's recurrent allusions to the constructive nature of concepts.[106] "Mach's influence was more direct and at the same time more complex."[337] Attempting to eliminate metaphysical elements from science, Mach concentrated his attention on the epistemological and methodological aspects of scientific research. Although not in sympathy with Mach's general philosophy of science, his critical writings appealed to Einstein's irrepressible sense of independence. Einstein's continuous striving for freedom of thought from the debilitating abuse of tradition had had very early origins.

The twelve years old Einstein had compared the contents of popular scientific books with those of biblical stories, and concluded that the latter were false. Thoroughly disillusioned, he became suspicious of all forms of authority and tradition. Parenthetically, throughout the centuries awakening young minds have abandoned the Christian faith at the impressionable age. They have turned to popular scientific books, often because of the responses of

Christians to their genuine openness and spirited inquiries. Defensive evasions, offensive condemnations, and extensive prohibitions were exclusively conservative and transparently authoritarian. Christianity is nothing, if not honest. Young minds should not be forced into the false dilemma of having to choose between faith and honesty.

Einstein, in particular, turned his back on what he regarded as intentional deception. The contemplation of the world seemed to offer freedom from an existence "dominated by wishes, hopes, and primitive feelings." It appeared to promise liberation from the chains of the "merely-personal."[112] This devastating experience left a profound and permanent impression with Einstein. It is readily detectable, for instance, in his address delivered at a celebration of Planck's sixtieth birthday.[70] Moreover, throughout Einstein's writings emphasis is repeatedly placed on both the rationality of the universe and the freedom of scientific researchers. Indeed, his scientific publications are monumental testimonies to what can be achieved when that freedom is subjected only to the pre-established harmony between thought and reality.

In this regard, Einstein found particularly acceptable Mach's criticism of Newton's ideas concerning space and time and his critical examination of Newtonian mechanics.[338] As he noted in his *Autobiographical Notes*, "I see Mach's greatness in his incorruptible skepticism and independence; in my younger years, however, Mach's epistemological position influenced me very greatly . . ."[133] Mach held "that facts by themselves can and should yield scientific knowledge without free conceptual construction."[213] Initially drawn by the force of Mach's critical thinking, Einstein was to learn as a working scientist that even Mach fell the victim of the corroboration and prolonged usage of scientific concepts. He misunderstood the status of the empirically given, "in consequence of which he condemned theory on precisely those points where its constructive-speculative character unconcealably comes to light, as for example in the kinetic atomic theory."[133] Einstein's reference to the kinetic atomic theory is surely non-arbitrary. By pointing directly to the beginnings of his productive scientific life, Einstein was specific about his "younger years."[59]

In his memorable paper of 1905 *On the Electrodynamics of Moving Bodies*[339], Einstein first presented a simple epistemological analysis of the concepts of space and time. Next, he defined simultaneity in terms of quantitative operational procedures dependent on the transmission of light signals. Einstein then discussed the relativity of lengths and times in the context of rigid rods, clocks, and moving bodies. A positivistic influence of Mach is not difficult to imagine, although to do so exclusively, one must overlook two formative postulates; the "principle of relativity" and the principle of the constancy of the velocity of light. The whole paper rests on those two principles. As "conceptual constructs" inaccessible to direct empirical confirmation, they are basically opposed to Mach's "anti-metaphysics." It is clear, then, that Einstein learned so well from Mach that he could not accept Mach's views uncritically. To use his own words, Einstein acted as an apparently "unscrupulous opportunist,"[50] subordinating the epistemological elements of his thought to the primary creativity of scientific thinking. Indeed, in his article on Bertrand Russell's theory of knowledge, he recorded that the immediate difficulties encountered in research, more than anything else, led him to his epistemological views.[5]

Fifth, Einstein's former mentor, Hermann Minkowski, a mathematician, re-interpreted the special theory of relativity. Using the concept of a four-dimensional pseudo-Euclidean geometry of space-time, he showed that the Lorentz transformations were the four-dimensional counterparts of rotations in three-dimensional space.[340] The new four-dimensional space accentuated the role of physical invariance. Minkowski's formalism provided a concise conceptual framework for the discussion of topics like simultaneity and causality. Its simple graphical representations of physical reality provided additional advantages. Rather than concentrating on the prominent operational aspects characteristic of Einstein's presentation, Minkowski used mathematics to simplify the description of the physical world. The four-dimensional space-time interval or vector ds seemed to point beyond measurement to axiomatics.[341] Consequently, Minkowski stressed that his apprehension of space-time had "sprung from the soil of experimental physics."[340]

The metaphysical elements of Minkowski's thought surfaced in the concluding sentence of his semi-popular lecture. He referred to "the idea of a pre-established harmony between pure mathematics and physics."[342] This correlation placed considerable emphasis on the value of constructive thought in general, and on Einstein's two postulates in particular. It also recognized a necessary role for empirical investigation. Obviously, when Einstein abandoned his own interpretation in favour of Minkowski's formulation, he moved deliberately against Mach's untenable epistemological position. Specifically, this strategy opposed Mach's doctrine that the laws of science are only summaries of experimental results. It is worth repeating however, that Einstein, as a working scientist, was never in sympathy with this dogma.

The importance of Minkowski's contribution was generously recorded by Einstein.[343] For him, it represented a concise in-course correction on his heuristic space-time journey to the general theory of relativity. As Gerald Whitrow commented, "Minkowski's fame today rests on his invention . . . of the concept of space-time, which had such a decisive influence on Einstein's development of general relativity, and is now recognized as one of the most important contributions ever made by a mathematician to natural philosophy."[344]

In reality, Einstein overcorrected. He became so strongly committed to Minkowski's space-time physics that he could recall forty years later how difficult it had been to leave the orbit of its influence. "The fact of the equality of inert and heavy mass thus leads quite naturally to the recognition that the basic demand of the special theory of relativity (invariance of the laws under Lorentz-transformations) is too narrow, i.e., that an invariance of the laws must be postulated also relative to *non-linear* transformations of the co-ordinates in the four-dimensional continuum. This happened in 1908. Why were another seven years required for the construction of the general theory of relativity? The main reason lies in the fact that it is not so easy to free oneself from the idea that co-ordinates must have an immediate metrical meaning."[345] Evidently, Einstein had first to liberate himself from what had acquired an undue authority over him, before he could effectively tackle the problem of universal gravitation. Minkowski's use of geometry to describe physical reality was, nevertheless, a directive to success.

In his *Notes on the Origin of the General Theory of Relativity*, Einstein explained, " . . . the inclusion of non-linear transformations, as the principle of equivalence demanded, was inevitably fatal to the simple physical interpretation of the co-ordinates – i.e., that it could no longer be required that co-ordinate differences should signify direct results of measurements with ideal scales or clocks. I was much bothered by this piece of knowledge, for it took me a long time to see what co-ordinates at all meant in physics. I did not find the way out of this dilemma until 1912 . . . The solution . . . was . . . as follows: A physical significance attaches not to the differentials of the co-ordinates but only to the Riemannian metric corresponding to them . . . I worked on these problems from 1912 to 1914 together with my friend [Marcel] Grossmann."[346] In fact, while this collaboration helped to convince Einstein that gravity was not a force but a property of space-time, he had yet to provide a satisfactory mathematical description.

There can be little doubt, therefore, that Minkowski's formulation had a profound effect on Einstein's scientific work and epistemological views. Indeed, Einstein implied as much in a letter to Cornelius Lanczos, dated January 24th 1938. "I began with a skeptical empiricism more or less like that of Mach. But the problem of gravitation converted me into a believing rationalist, that is, into someone who searches for the only reliable source of Truth in mathematical simplicity."[347] There was not, of course, an instantaneous conversion, only a growing sympathy with the natural order because of the pre-established harmony between thought and reality.[347]

Banesh Hoffmann asked and answered the all-important question. "What were the seeds that gave rise to (the) wonderfully unique structure (of the general theory of relativity)? Such things as Newton's theory, and the special theory of relativity of course, and Minkowski's idea of a four-dimensional world, and Mach's powerful criticisms of Newton's theory. Also the mathematical framework already prepared [in collaboration with Grossman, and built by Karl Gauss, Wolfgang Bolyai, Nikolai Lobachevski, Bernhard Riemann, Elwin Christoffel, William Clifford, Gregario Ricci and Tullio Levi-Civita]. But after that what? The principle of equivalence, the principle of general covariance, and – why, essentially nothing else."[348]

A galaxy of mathematicians had prepared the way for Einstein. How could he ever turn his back on scientific continuity and learning? With many "years of anxious searching in the dark"[346] behind him, Einstein had been painfully persuaded that "knowledge exists in two forms – lifeless, stored in books, and alive in the consciousness of men. The second form of existence is after all the essential one; the first, indispensable as it may be, occupies only an inferior position."[349] A generation before Einstein, Riemann had invented a geometry of curved surfaces logically independent of any physical basis. Einstein had taken it from the "books," used it to represent a law of motion, and provided a theory that excited the scientific world. Besides, while the Newtonian view of space as a passive container is rejected in both theories of relativity, the general theory endows space with physical qualities due to the interdependence of gravity and matter. This correlation of mathematics and physical reality re-introduced the notion of an "ether." With the cat once again among the pigeons, Einstein's theory was very much alive in the consciousness of scientists. Einstein's epistemological perspective was oriented by his working life as a scientist. Indeed, it was firmly rooted in, and grew out of, his scientific apprehension and experience.

In the opening remarks of his *Autobiographical Notes*, Einstein warned his readers that "the exposition of that which is worthy of communication does nonetheless not come easy – today's person of 67 is by no means the same as was the one of 50, of 30, of 20. Every reminiscence is coloured by today's being what it is, and therefore by a deceptive point of view."[350] Several paragraphs later, readers are reminded of the misting of memory by intervening experiences. "In this case it is well possible that such an individual in retrospect sees a uniformly systematic development, whereas the actual experience takes place in kaleidoscopic particular situations."[112] Advancing only a few more pages, one learns that Einstein's epistemological "credo actually evolved only much later and very slowly and does not correspond with the point of view I held in younger years."[59]

Einstein's repeated references to the tricks played on memory by experience hint at the strength of his conviction that the working life of a scientist moulds his epistemological views. In his *Reply to Criticisms* he addressed the subject directly. "The reciprocal relationship of epistemology and science is of noteworthy kind. They are dependent upon each other. Epistemology without contact with science becomes an empty scheme. Science without epistemology is – in so far as it is thinkable at all – primitive and muddled. However, no sooner has the epistemologist, who is seeking a clear system, fought his way through to such a system than he is inclined to interpret the thought-content of science in the sense of his system and to reject whatever does not fit into his system. The scientist, however, cannot afford to carry his striving for epistemological systematic that far."[189] Scientists cannot serve two masters. Therefore scientific researchers give pride of place to the intuitive relation. Epistemology takes a lesser but important position.

"Nobody who has really gone deeply into the matter will deny that in practice the world of phenomena uniquely determines the theoretical system, in spite of the fact that there is no logical bridge between the world of phenomena and their theoretical principles; this is what Leibnitz described so happily as a "pre-established harmony." Physicists often accuse epistemologists of not paying sufficient attention to this fact."[111] "This fact" represented the fulcrum of Einstein's epistemological lever.

He believed that scientists are guided by and subject to the rationality of the universe. In so far as they are open to the natural order, scientists increase their apprehension. In Einstein's figurative words, "the liberty of choice, however, is a special kind; it is not in any way similar to the liberty of the writer of fiction. Rather it is similar to that of a man engaged in solving a well designed word puzzle. He may, it is true, propose any word as a solution; but, there is only one word which really solves the puzzle in all its forms."[154] Scientists strive to remain obedient to the pre-established harmony of thought and reality. They manage it within the limitations of their apprehension and experience.

There is, therefore, abundant evidence to support the simple conclusion that Einstein's comments on epistemological aspects of scientific research were grounded in personal, patient, and profound labour and activity. In fact, his essays on scientific research only began to appear after he had produced both the special and general theories of relativity. Einstein could "see, on the one side, the totality of sense experiences, and, on the other, the totality of the concepts and propositions which are laid down in books."[59] He could see, on the one hand, the totality of scientific experience, and, on the other, the totality of epistemological and methodological propositions. The two hands had to be intuitively clasped to yield a consistent, open and therefore incomplete description of nature, of which he was a little part. Specifically, Einstein rejected abstraction which led to Newtonian physics for the intuitive relation which had taken him to the special and general theories. He avoided epistemological systems. He believed that a scientist should be, first and foremost, scientific in his thinking. Only scientific answers should be given by a scientist to questions on scientific thinking.

21. SCIENCE AND RELIGION

The metaphysical significance of space-time has been discussed by many Christians since the appearance of Einstein's special theory of relativity in 1905. In fact, this theory has a particular fascination for those interested in the mystery of time. In classical physics, space is described as a three dimensional Euclidean continuum. It is homogeneous and isotropic. Very few people have difficulty with the concept of the distance between Princeton and Bethlehem, but how many can make any sense of the corresponding interval between Princeton now and Bethlehem at the moment of Jesus' birth? The spatio-temporal interval between spacially separated, non-simultaneous events is not even a quantitative concept in classical physics. Space and time are measured in disparate units.

The invariance of the velocity of light (c) renders the results of spatial and temporal measurement comparable in relativistic physics. Time intervals can be multiplied by c to obtain space-like intervals. The resulting intervals of space-time have the same value for all observers. The spatial and temporal measurements are relative to the state of motion of the observer. There are no absolute juxapositions nor are two events simultaneous for one observer also simultaneous for another. Nevertheless, this scientific theory does not dispense with the distinctive characteristics of space and time. Neither is reducible to the other.

Indeed, Einstein's special theory, like Newton's edifice, has the powerfully heuristic quality of obvious multiple connectivity as the interpretations of Einstein and Minkowski illustrate. Besides, the diversity of interpretations is even more marked in the case of the general theory of relativity. There is nothing internal to the special theory that proves one particular interpretation to be unconditionally superior. On the contrary, it was largely Einstein's search for a more general theory that encouraged him to adopt Minkowski's formulation. Moreover, the laws of classical and relativistic physics are causal in much the same sense. In the latter, an infinite set of contemporary events is always irrelevant to the prediction of any particular event, whereas in the former, all events are obscurely relevant in principle.

Einstein responded to the interpretative uncertainties by relying on scientific criteria, or rather the intuitive relation. Otherwise he would have opened the flood-gate of unbridled speculation. His reservations about epistemological systems had "sprung from the soil of experimental physics."[340] Clearly, without a basic understanding of relativistic physics, Christians must depend on hearsay or blind chance. Yet such an understanding reveals that there is no unique path from relativistic physics to theology.

As already noted, Einstein used the concept of "cosmic religious feeling" to explain his motivation in science. He believed that this "feeling is the strongest and noblest motive for scientific research,"[246] but that "it can give rise to no definite notion of God and no theology."[247] Einstein was frank about his unusual religious views. "A knowledge of the existence of something we cannot penetrate, of the manifestations of the profoundest reason and the most radiant beauty, which are only accessible to our reason in their most elementary forms – it is this knowledge and this emotion that constitute the truly religious attitude; in this sense, and in this alone, I am a deeply religious man."[351] In fact, he could not conceive of a genuine scientist without a profound faith "in the possibility that the regulations valid for the world of existence are rational, that is, comprehensible to reason."[352]

The cosmic religious feeling is intimately associated with belief in an external world independent of the perceiving subject as the basis of all natural science.[63] Einstein depended on the past faithfulness of the rationality of the universe while exercising his creative faculties. Without this faithfulness, the motivation of the scientist is chaotic and tends to fade simply because it cannot deepen by virtue of experience, struggle and growth. Alternatively, motivation almost devoid of creativity does not progress far beyond learning. When both faithfulness and creativity are held together, the scientist experiences what Einstein meant by "the cosmic religious feeling" which is grounded in the inseparability of "the empirical and rational components of knowledge."

According to Einstein, the scientific enterprise requires such faith because " . . . mere thinking cannot give us a sense of the ultimate and fundamental ends. To make clear these fundamental ends and valuations, and to set them fast in the emotional life of the individual, seem(ed to Einstein) precisely the most important function which religion has to perform in the social life of man."[129] Einstein's scientific life illustrates how the belief of the scientist can strengthen commitment to and interpret this religious feeling. Although he seems to have used the terms passionate devotion,[282] unselfish desire,[103] passion for comprehension,[148] and cosmic religious feeling more or less interchangeably, different aspects of the last are accentuated by the other three. The cosmic religious feeling sets itself apart from objectivism or dispassionate neutrality, subjectivism or selfish desires and extreme rationalism or unimpassioned understanding. Its aim is progressive liberation from the disunity of everyday experiences.[353] The vehicle that carries the scientist to freedom is the self-discipline of scientific standards of research powered by preoccupation with superpersonal validity. "Certain it is that a conviction, akin to religious feeling, of the rationality or intelligibility of the world lies behind all scientific work of a higher order."[120]

The law of causality, according to Einstein, rules supreme in the universe. He even assumed that life, itself, would be deducible from it.[111] Presently, life is known to obey "the rule of fixed necessity."[166] Indeed, "the more a man is imbued with the ordered regularity of all events, the firmer becomes his conviction that there is no room left by the side of this ordered regularity for causes of a different nature. For him, neither the rule of human nor the rule of divine will exists as an independent cause of natural events."[354] Einstein regarded "the universal operation of the law of causation"[246] as convincingly illustrated by the "organic development of Newton's ideas"[258] across the centuries. Its operation is the will of God,[129] the revelation of the mind of God. Undoubtedly, Einstein's thoughts on God's omnipotence were greatly influenced by his knowledge of the implications of the defects of Newton's edifice and his own scientific theories. A transcendent God who expresses his omnipotence in such terms is neither "a Being who interferes in the course of human events"[246] nor One who "exists as an independent cause of natural events,"[7] nor One who acts instantaneously at a distance.

Einstein could not reconcile his views on causality with the notion of a "personal" God who grants human petitions.[352] Besides, a God who is "personally" active in the world as a causal agent is, in Einstein's view, radically implicated in the problem of evil.[352] Einstein's God is not. His will is eternally expressed in terms of causal invariance which caters for the decisions of the individual. Einstein believed that man can be freed from fear of God and the struggle for personal salvation, freed to become "religious" in a cosmic sense. Einstein seems to have intellectualized the religious quest to a quasi-scientific enterprise, a rational form consistent with, but not equivalent to, the scientific endeavour. Indeed, he revealed his priorities with the remark, "science without religion is lame, religion without science is blind."[266]

From an Einsteinian perspective, the basic conflict between science and religion arises from the incompatibility of anthropomorphic conceptions of God and "the universal operation of the law of causation."[103] Fundamentally, science and religion tackle different tasks. While science "is the attempt of the posterior reconstruction of existence by the process of conceptualization,"[103] religion deals only with the moral, ethical and emotional life of individuals.[103] Einstein was convinced that " . . . science can only ascertain what *is,* but not what *should be,* and outside of its domain value judgments of all kinds remain necessary. Religion, on the other hand, deals only with evaluations of human thought and action; it cannot justifiably speak of facts and relationships between facts."[6] False conflicts between science and religion commonly spring from "fatal errors" that confuse these distinctive functions.[6] Nevertheless, "scientific method itself would not have led anywhere, it would not even have been born without a passionate striving for clear understanding."[355] Evidently, Einstein was not sufficiently motivated to pursue the problems associated with the concept of a superpersonal Being. As a scientist, he focused his attention on the inexhaustible difficulties of apprehending the revelation of that superior Mind.

In so many respects, Einstein appears to have stood before the threshold of the Christian faith. The incompleteness of his utterances of religious, epistemological and scientific content demonstrates the penetrating consistency of Einstein's scientific thinking. It also shows how the scientific enterprise can lead the scientific researcher to the question, "Why think theologically?" Scientific endeavour, however, cannot provide the motivation necessary to pursue the theological quest. This desire must come from a different direction. Nevertheless, a healthy regard for theological thinking can be generated by scientific thinking as illustrated by Einstein's reluctance to borrow supposedly well-known theological terms. In fact, many scientists attempt to answer the question, "Why think theologically?" If they have learned from Einstein, they might even take the study of theology too seriously for many fellow Christians.[356]

22. OPENNESS AND JUSTIFICATION

An outstanding feature common to all of Einstein's remarks is openness to an independent physical world. Einstein explained his views on gravitation in characteristically lucid terms. "It is sufficient – as far as we know – for the representation of the observed facts of celestial mechanics. But it is similar to a building, one wing of which is made of fine marble (left part of the equation), but the other wing is built of low grade wood (right side of the equation). The phenomenological representation of matter is, in fact, only a crude substitute for a representation which would do justice to all known properties of matter."[357] The equation in question relates the Riemannian geometry of space-time to the energy-momentum tensor of distributed matter and energy. Einstein expressed his dissatisfaction with the general theory of relativity by indicating where he believed its weakness lay. He maintained that the mathematical treatment of space-time is essentially "the right way" to proceed. Nevertheless, by his reckoning, a great deal of work had still to be done on the representation of matter before the scientific house could be put in proper order.

Clearly, Einstein was as eager to have his own theories improved, as he was to see beyond those of other scientists. According to Otto Frisch, a pioneer of nuclear fission, "When anybody contradicted him [Einstein] he thought it over and if he found he was wrong he was delighted, because he felt that he had escaped from an error and that now he knew better than before. For the same reason he never hesitated to change his opinion when he found that he had made a mistake and to say so."[358] The incident with Lanczos is a good example (vide supra). The reactions of most scientists do not quite match Einstein's unqualified devotion to the pursuit of truth. He was convinced, for instance, that "as far as propositions of mathematics refer to reality, they are not certain, and as far as they are certain, they do not refer to reality."[359] Such insights entrenched his determination to remain open to the intuitive faculties of other scientists. The research courses run by scientists are heavily fenced with likelihoods. Conjointly, they jump the unknown and unexpected in thinking and doing. Where possible, they avoid the handicaps of unbridled speculation and blinkered certainty.

Einstein's Herbert Spencer Lecture On the Method of Theoretical Physics,[360] was delivered at Oxford in 1933. He raised the question of the non-logical relation of the sense experiences and freely invented concepts. As he did so, his uncompromising commitment to the openness of scientific thinking was never more obvious. "Can we hope to be guided safely by experience at all when there exist theories (such as classical mechanics) which to a large extent do justice to experience, without getting to the root of the matter? I answer without hesitation that there is, in my opinion, a right way, and that we are capable of finding it. Our experience hitherto justifies us in believing that nature is the realization of the simplest conceivable mathematical ideas. I am convinced that we can discover by means of purely mathematical constructions the concepts and laws connecting them with each other, which furnish the key to the understanding of natural phenomena."[360] Of course, the inseparability of the empirical and rational components of knowledge ensures that even "purely" mathematical constructions are empirically loaded.

Einstein answered the question, "Why think scientifically?" A scientist ought to think scientifically because it is his most effective way to increase humankind's apprehension of the natural order. Adapting Brown's words, this answer has no force unless it is assumed that a scientist ought to pursue this goal.[267] Einstein knew that the pursuit of science was ultimately a matter of faith. He said so repeatedly. His "nose" for truth was precious to him. Obviously, he accepted this goal and also the imperative that a scientist ought to pursue it. According to him, the sole justification for a scientific thought, statement, or theory resides in the inherent rationality of the universe. It may become part of the corporate experience of the scientific community, but it always originates as personal scientific experience.

As scientists stand open to the structured world, they abandon notions of final solutions to scientific problems and epistemological systems.[70] Bondi, for example, believes that vain strivings "at ultimate equations, to come to ultimate final complete statements, to theories unifying all that we know . . . is a very dangerous tendency . . ."[361] In equally general terms, Einstein and Infeld suggested that "a complete solution [to the mystery of the universe] seems to recede as we advance."[362] Scientists have to live with an unfinished view of the universe. They will never cease to ask new questions. Hopefully, they will continue to be confronted with new discoveries and problems. The endless quest of science is a candid search for apprehension, not comprehension. "To obtain even a partial solution the scientist must collect unordered facts available and make them coherent and understandable by creative thought."[363]

Einstein never saw himself as a philosopher.[364] With his great gifts he found the most important scientific questions. Faithful to his intuited beliefs, he pursued those questions without losing contact with the main problems. If, in the process, he could contribute occasionally to epistemology, then there was no harm in that. But he never allowed himself to be side-tracked by a search for a logic of scientific research. Einstein devoted his life to research *in* science. His commitment was to much more than a prescribed scientific methodology. He knew scientific research to be greater than the sum of all scientific methods as laid down in books. His apprehension exceeded intuitively the articulated content of science. To borrow his own words, nothing can be said concerning the detailed manner in which scientific thinking is to be accomplished and refined, and how it is to be co-ordinated to experience,[151] only that it is alive in the consciousness of the scientific researcher.[349.] Einstein's "credo," presented in his "obituary," testifies to the openness of scientific thinking. In fact, it reads rather like an epistemological parallel to the description of his general theory of relativity.[59] This association of ideas and its like lay behind his repeated warnings to the reader in the early paragraphs of his *Autobiographical Notes*. In this contribution, Einstein stated plainly that "actual (scientific) experience takes place in kaleidoscopic particular situations,"[107] not in accordance with an algorithm.

Elsewhere, Einstein commented, "If you want to find out anything from the theoretical physicists about the methods they use, I advise you to stick closely to one principle: don't listen to their words, fix your attention on their deeds."[97] He did not mean, however, that a scientist's description of scientific procedures is totally unreliable. Nor was he implying that only observations and experiments are worthy of consideration. Certainly, there are some people who teach such things, but they miss the very point that Einstein took pains to make. As Filmer Northop indicated, Einstein was far too good a scientist, too profound a thinker, to forget for one moment the mystery of the inseparability of the empirical and theoretical components of knowledge.[365] This mystery, for example, lies at the heart of the general theory of relativity and at the core of determinate nature. That is why Einstein prefaced the above advice with the following statement. "To him who is a discoverer in this field [theoretical physics], the products of his imagination appear as so necessary and natural that he regards them, and would like to have them regarded by others, not as creations of thought but as given realities."[97]

Einstein was primarily concerned about the tendency among scientists to forget the intuitive connections of their theories to the physical world. The inclination to regard them as empirically given increased through sheer force of habit. To understand scientific thinking one must look behind the words of the scientific researcher to the theories of the natural sciences, to their concepts, and to the methods actually used by scientists. Those are the "deeds" to which Einstein referred as he raised the fundamental problem of belief in scientific thinking. Basically, Einstein was suggesting that anyone sufficiently interested in scientific research should get down to concrete cases. As previously noted, it is not what is heard and said by spectators or critics that carries research along, but the labour and activity of scientists.[366] That labour and activity includes the logically free creations of scientific minds.

Einstein admitted freely that the scientist "must appear to the systematic epistemologist as a type of unscrupulous opportunist: he appears as *realist* in so far as he seeks to describe a world independent of acts of perception; as *idealist* in so far as he looks upon the concepts and theories as free inventions of the human spirit . . .; as *positivist* in so far as he considers his concepts and theories justified only to the extent to which they furnish a logical representation of relations among sensory experiences."[50] The ease with which selected aspects of scientific thinking can be associated with diverse philosophical traditions hints at the subordinate role of epistemology in scientific thinking. It sheds some light on how a scientist can appear to be philosophically inconsistent, while remaining scientifically rational. It also helps to explain how scientists can function effectively despite individual allegiances to the spectra of modern philosophies and theologies. Lastly, it indicates how many Christians can be misled by the appearance of scientific thinking as both confused and ill-founded. It cannot, however, exonerate them from the charges of premature judgment and ignorance of the "deeds" of scientists.

Actually, Christians should be especially reluctant to draw such conclusions for they have to come to terms with similar circumstances. A prominent feature of modern Christian theology is that it does not address univocally contemporary confrontations of culture and technology. The prevalent inconsistencies and ambiguities reflect a whole range of so-called theological thinking. At one extreme, biblical representations or images are taken as mere conventions with no anchorage in the objective Reality of God as revealed in the Person of Jesus Christ, the Lord and Saviour of the world. Their significance relies exclusively on the presuppositions and desires of the particular individual. At the opposite extreme, biblical statements are seized as pictorial representations or models to be exhaustively studied and rigorously applied. Yet beyond their arbitrary encapsulation of biblical "truths," they are detached from all creative reference. On the one hand, many Christians are threatened by subversive superficiality and, on the other hand, numerous believers risk slavery to evacuated objectivism. Only as Christians allow their presuppositions and desires to be creatively questioned by the objective Reality of God can they hope to transcend idiosyncratic interpretations and incoherent rationalizations.

Apparently, the inseparability of the theoretical and empirical components of knowledge, the divergent views among scientists on particular methods and theories, and the complexity of scientific thinking are problems which have counterparts in modern theology. They should strike chords of sympathy as they remind Christians of the domestic frailties and strengths of modern theological thinking. In neither case, however, is the face of adversity quite sufficient to arrest the pursuit of appropriate personal beliefs.

It is not the business of scientists to become bogged down in epistemological details or to qualify scientific beliefs out of existence. Bondi first gave Newton's second law as an example of an open theoretical statement based on the available data. Then he wrote, "It is an essential part of science that (a scientist) be able to describe matters in a way where he can say something without knowing everything."[367] "All science is full of statements where you put the best face on your ignorance, where you say: true enough, we know awfully little about this, but more or less irrespective of the stuff that we don't know about, we can make certain useful deductions."[368] As long as scientists operate meaningfully within a broad basic framework of scientific beliefs, their precise methods of inquiry are largely determined by the detailed nature of current research activities. In the laboratory or at the office, it is not a question of confusion or ill-founded methods. Personal intuitions and evaluations meet the standards, but not necessarily the immediate support, of the wider scientific community. In the long run, they must, of course, speak persuasively to that community.

Every research scientist practises conceptual "parsimony" by every method he can. Scientists have no inviolable epistemological principles, but on occasions they will defend every one of them.

Many scientists worship in church at weekends and with their researches for the rest of the week. With rare exceptions, they are self-disciplined researchers who delight in their own logically free creations. Briefly, scientific researchers strive as scientific realists to advance scientific theories.

In particular, Einstein cautiously limited himself to the field of physics.[5] He had no new scientific method to propound, no novel comprehensive epistemology to offer, and no startling proof that scientific theories or statements are indubitable. This brilliant scientist rejected both scepticism and idealism. He believed in an independent reality which he could see only dimly. On the basis of his scientific wisdom and well over forty years ago, Albert Einstein provided a scientific answer, a realistic, coherent open reply, to the question, "Why think scientifically?" Perhaps surprisingly, his answer raises the question, "Why think theologically?", but a responsible reply to it would require another essay.

23. NOTES

1. The reading of H. I. Brown's recent paper, *"On Being Rational,"* *American Philosophical Quarterly, 15,* p. 241 (1978), prompted the writing of this essay.
2. A. Einstein, *Ideas and Opinions,* translated Sonja Bargmann, LONDON: Souvenir Press, 1973, p. 16.
3. G. Holton, *Thematic Origins of Scientific Thought: Kepler to Einstein,* CAMBRIDGE and LONDON: Harvard University Press, 1973, p. 459.
4. M. Caulley and A. Tétry in *A Random Walk in Science,* compiled R. L .Weber and edited E. Mendoza, LONDON and BRISTOL: The Institute of Physics, 1973, p. 47.
5. *Ideas and Opinions,* p. 19.
6. *Ibid.,* p. 45. See also K. Gauthen, *Zygon, 1,* p. 256 (1966).
7. *Ibid.,* p. 48.
8. G. Thomson, *The Inspiration of Science,* NEW YORK: Anchor Books, 1968, p. vii.
9. *Thematic Origins,* p. 449.
10. *Ibid.,* p. 450.
11. W. Cooper in *Random Walk,* p. vii.
12. *Ideas and Opinions,* p. 15.
13. M. Born, *Physics in my generation,* LONDON: Heidelberg Science Library, 1970, p. 125.
14. *Thematic Origins,* p. 446.
15. *Ibid.,* p. 462.
16. *Ibid.,* p. 393.
17. *My generation,* p. 71.
18. *Ibid.,* p. 100.
19. *Thematic Origins,* p. 237.
20. H. Bondi, *Assumption and Myth in Physical Theory,* CAMBRIDGE: Cambridge University Press, 1967, p. 2.
21. *Ibid.,* p. 3.
22. *Thematic Origins,* p. 406.
23. L. M. Branscomb, *American Scientist, 61,* p. 39 (1973).
24. W. J. Kaufmann, *Relativity and Cosmology,* NEW YORK: Harper Row, 1977, pp. 1f.
25. *Thematic Origins,* p. 452.
26. *Ideas and Opinions,* p. 31.
27. *Thematic Origins,* p. 456.
28. E. Nagel, *Humanist, 36,* p. 34 (1976).
29. *Ibid.,* p. 35. See also *Ideas and Opinions,* p. 221.
30. *Ibid.,* p. 36.
31. *Ibid.,* p. 37.
32. N. Bohr in *Random Walk,* p. 14.
33. M. Polanyi, *Science, Faith and Society,* CHICAGO and LONDON: The University of Chicago Press, 1964, p. 33.

34. B. Magee, *Karl Popper*, NEW YORK: The Viking Press, 1973, pp. 1f.
35. *Thematic Origins*, p. 382.
36. *Ideas and Opinions*, p. 221.
37. *Thematic Origins*, p. 385.
38. W. I. Beveridge, *The Art of Scientific Investigation*, LONDON: Heinemann, 1961, pp. 160-8. See also *Ideas and Opinions*, pp. 359f and 253-61.
39. A. M. Taylor, *Imagination and The Growth of Science*, NEW YORK: Schocken Books, 1967, p. 1.
40. S. C. Brown, *Zygon, 1*, p. 16 (1966).
41. *Assumption and Myth*, p. 3. See also p. 8.
42. N. Reschner, *Scientific Progress*, OXFORD: Basil Blackwell, 1978, pp. 234-45.
43. G. Gore, quoted *Scientific Progress*, pp. 244f.
44. A. Einstein and L. Infeld, *The Evolution of Physics*, NEW YORK: Simon and Schuster, 1938, p. 75.
45. *Ibid.*, pp. 151f.
46. *Ibid.*, pp. 296f.
47. *The Born-Einstein Letters*, translated Irene Born, LONDON and BASINGSTOKE: Macmillan Press, 1971, p. 71.
48. *Evolution of Physics*, p. 26.
49. *Ideas and Opinions*, p. 284.
50. A. Einstein in *Albert Einstein: Philosopher-Scientist*, edited P. A. Schlipp, NEW YORK: Tudor Publishing Company, 1951, p. 684.
51. *Ideas and Opinions*, p. 25.
52. *On Being Rational*, p. 242.
53. R. V. Jones in *Random Walk*, p. 9.
54. G. J. Whitrow, *Philosophical Journal, 14*, p. 70 (1977).
55. H. Bondi in *Problems of Scientific Revolutions*, edited R. Harré, OXFORD: Clarendon Press, 1975, p. 3.
56. *Philosophical Journal*, p. 76.
57. *My generation*, p. 166.
58. I. Newton, quoted *Random Walk*, p. 203.
59. *Philosopher-Scientist*, pp. 11f.
60. G. Holton, *The Scientific Imagination: Case Studies*, LONDON, NEW YORK and MELBOURNE: Cambridge University Press, 1978, p. 233. See also *Ideas and Opinions*, pp. 8-11.
61. *My generation*, p. 169.
62. A. Einstein, *Out of My Later Years*, NEW YORK: Philosophical Library, 1950, p. 223.
63. *Ideas and Opinions*, pp. 24 and 266.
64. *My generation*, p. 146.
65. *Scientific Imagination*, p. 230.
66. *My generation*, p. 147.
67. *Scientific Imagination*, pp. 234 and 245.
68. H. Bondi in *Perspectives in Quantum Theory*, CAMBRIDGE and LONDON: The M.I.T. Press, 1971, p. 238.

69. A. Einstein in Foreword to L. BARNETT, *The Universe and Dr Einstein*, NEW YORK: Bantam Books, 1968, p. 9.
70. *Ideas and Opinions*, pp. 225f.
71. P. H. Abelson, *Science, 194*, p. 565 (1976).
72. E. P. Wigner in *Random Walk*, p. 201.
73. *My generation*, p. 88.
74. *Relativity and Cosmology*, pp. 53-6.
75. *Scientific Imagination*, p. 241.
76. *My generation*, p. 109.
77. *Scientific Imagination*, p. 85.
78. *Ibid.*, p. 243.
79. H. Dingle in *Einstein: the man and his achievement*, edited G. J. Whitrow, NEW YORK: Dover Publications, 1973, p. 7.
80. *Scientific Imagination*, p. 246.
81. E. Straus in *Einstein: the man*, pp. 77f.
82. *Scientific Imagination*, pp. 238 and 241.
83. *Inspiration of Science*, p. 20.
84. R. L. Weber in *Random Walk*, p. xv.
85. *Inspiration of Science*, p. 11.
86. A. S. Russell in *Random Walk*, p. 50.
87. L. Boltzmann, quoted *Random Walk*, p. 43.
88. *Scientific Imagination*, pp. 245 and 248.
89. *Ibid.*, p. 250.
90. *Thematic Origins*, p. 463.
91. P. Bergmann in *Einstein: the man*, pp. 73 and 88.
92. *Philosopher-Scientist*, p. 17.
93. *Ideas and Opinions*, pp. 289f.
94. A. Einstein, quoted by E. G. Straus in *Einstein: A Centenary Volume*, edited A. P. French, CAMBRIDGE: Harvard University Press, 1979, p. 31.
95. G. J. Whitrow in *Einstein: the man*, p. 7.
96. A. Einstein, quoted *A Centenary Volume*, p. 113.
97. *Ibid.*, p. 310.
98. *Later Years*, p. 59. See also *On Being Rational*, p. 247.
99. *Ibid.*, p. 60.
100. *Ibid.*, p. 63.
101. *Ibid.*, p. 64.
102. This particular expression was first used by N. R. Hanson, *Patterns of Discovery: An Enquiry into the Conceptual Foundations of Science*, NEW YORK: Cambridge University Press, 1968. See Einstein's use of the word "empirical" in his essays on "Johannes Kepler" and "The Mechanics of Newton and their Influence on the Development of Theoretical Physics" in *Ideas and Opinions*, pp. 262-6 and 253-61.
103. *Ideas and Opinions*, p. 44.
104. *Ibid.*, pp. 271ff. and V. F. Lenzen, *Philosopher-Scientist*, p. 361.
105. A. Einstein, *Relativity, The Special and General Theories*, translated R. W. Lawson, WHITSTABLE: Latimer Trend, 1960, pp. 141f.

106. *Ideas and Opinions*, pp. 22f.
107. *Philosopher-Scientist*, p. 7.
108. *Ideas and Opinions*, pp. 25f.
109. *Ibid.*, p. 9.
110. *Thematic Origins*, pp. 386f.
111. *Ideas and Opinions*, p. 226.
112. *Philosopher-Scientist*, pp. 5f.
113. *Ibid.*, pp. 7-9.
114. *Later Years*, pp. 62f.
115. *Philosopher-Scientist*, pp. 11f and *Ideas and Opinions*, pp. 25f.
116. *Ideas and Opinions*, p. 277.
117. A. Einstein in *Albert Einstein: The Human Side*, edited Helen Dukas and B. Hoffman, PRINCETON: Princeton University Press, 1979, p. 29.
118. *Ideas and Opinions*, pp. 221f., *Philosopher-Scientist*, p. 27 and *Thematic Origins*, p. 109.
119. *Ideas and Opinions*, p. 282.
120. *Ibid.*, p. 262.
121. *Later Years*, pp. 59f.
122. *Ibid.*, p. 224.
123. *Ideas and Opinions*, p. 263.
124. *Ibid.*, p. 264.
125. *Later Years*, p. 225.
126. *Ideas and Opinions*, p. 265.
127. *Later Years*, p. 226.
128. *Ideas and Opinions*, p. 266.
129. *Ibid.*, p. 42.
130. V. F. Lenzen in *Philosopher-Scientist*, p. 363 and *Ideas and Opinions*, p. 226.
131. H. Minkowski in H. A. Lorentz *et al*, *The Principle of Relativity*, translated W. Perrett and G. B. Jeffery, NEW YORK: Dover Publications, 1923, p. 91.
132. *Thematic Origins*, pp. 204-6 and *Ideas and Opinions*, p. 226.
133. *Philosopher-Scientist*, pp. 21f.
134. *Thematic Origins*, pp. 189f and 234f and *Scientific Imagination*, pp. 97f and footnote 30.
135. A. Einstein, *Jahrbuch der Radioaktivität und Elektronik, 4*, pp. 411-62 (1907).
136. W. Kaufmann, *Annalen der Physik, 49*, pp. 487-553 (1906).
137. *On Being Rational*, p. 243.
138. K. R. Popper, *Conjectures and Refutations*, LONDON: Routledge and Kegan Paul, 1972, pp. 114f.
139. K. R. Popper, *The Logic of Scientific Discovery*, LONDON: Hutchinson and Co. Ltd., 1959, p. 32.
140. *Ibid.*, p. 40.
141. *Conjectures and Refutations*, pp. 215ff.
142. *On Being Rational*, p. 245.

143. *Philosopher-Scientist*, p. 33.
144. *Ibid.*, pp. 15f.
145. *Ibid.*, p. 19.
146. *Ideas and Opinions*, p. 287.
147. W. B. Bonner in *Einstein: the man*, p. 66.
148. *Ideas and Opinions*, p. 342.
149. *Ibid.*, p. 352.
150. *Ibid.*, p. 11.
151. *Later Years*, p. 61.
152. *Thematic Origins*, p. 190. See also pp. 47–66.
153. M. Born in *Philosopher-Scientist*, p. 177.
154. *Later Years*, p. 64.
155. G. Holton in *A Centenary Volume*, p. 159. See also *Later Years*, p. 61.
156. *Later Years*, pp. 60f.
157. R. V. Jones in *Random Walk*, p. 10.
158. *My Generation*, p. 15.
159. V. Berezinsky in *Random Walk*, p. 97.
160. V. F. Lenzen in *Philosopher-Scientist*, p. 359. See also *Later Years*, p. 69.
161. A. Einstein, quoted by M. Born in *Philosopher-Scientist*, p. 196.
162. *Ideas and Opinions*, p. 258. See Holton's discussions in *Thematic Origins*, pp. 47–66 and *Scientific Imagination*, pp. 99f.
163. T. S. Kuhn, *The Structure of Scientific Revolutions*, CHICAGO: University of Chicago Press, 1970.
164. *Assumption and Myth*, pp. 56–60.
165. *Born-Einstein Letters*, p. 91.
166. *Ideas and Opinions*, p. 47.
167. *Ibid.*, p. 49.
168. *Philosopher-Scientist*, p. 13.
169. *Ideas and Opinions*, pp. 261f.
170. *The Human Side*, p. 18.
171. A. Einstein, quoted by V. G. Hinshaw Jr., in *Philosopher-Scientist*, p. 650.
172. *Ideas and Opinions*, p. 12.
173. A. Einstein, quoted by The New York Times, April 27th, 1921.
174. *Ideas and Opinions*, p. 40.
175. *Evolution of Physics*, p. 296.
176. *Ideas and Opinions*, p. 33.
177. *Thematic Origins*, p. 15.
178. H. Bondi in *Problems of Scientific Revolutions*, pp. 7f.
179. A. Einstein, quoted in *A Centenary Volume*, p. 245.
180. *Ideas and Opinions*, p. 224.
181. *Later Years*, p. 32f.
182. *Ideas and Opinions*, p. 64.
183. *On Being Rational*, p. 246.
184. E. H. Hutten in *Einstein: the man*, p. 52.
185. *My generation*, p. 25.
186. *Ibid.*, p. 145.

187. L. M. Branscomb, *loc cit.*, p. 38.
188. *My generation*, p. 108.
189. *Philosopher-Scientist*, pp. 683f.
190. *Later Years*, p. 33.
191. C. Sykes in *Einstein: the man*, p. ix.
192. *Thematic Origins*, p. 116.
193. *Imagination and Growth*, p. 25.
194. *Ibid.*, pp. 60f. See also *My generation*, pp. 22 and 71.
195. E. Rutherford, quoted *Inspiration of Science*, p. 61.
196. *Imagination and Growth*, p. 70. See also *My generation*, p. 76.
197. *Philosopher-Scientist*, p. 47.
198. M. Born in *Philosopher-Scientist*, p. 163.
199. A. Einstein, *Annalen der Physik*, *17*, pp. 132–48 (1905).
200. H. R. Hertz, *Electric Waves*, translated D. Jones, LONDON: Macmillan, 1893, pp. 63ff.
201. *Evolution of Physics*, p. 259.
202. *My generation*, p. 24.
203. M. Klein in *A Centenary Volume*, pp. 104f.
204. M. Born in *Philosopher-Scientist*, p. 167.
205. J. C. Maxwell, *Treatise on Electricity and Magnetism*, OXFORD: Clarendon Press, 1873.
206. *Evolution of Physics*, p. 143.
207. B. Hoffman in collaboration with Helen Dukas, *Albert Einstein: Creator and Rebel*, NEW YORK: Viking Press, 1972, p. 54.
208. A. Einstein, *Annalen der Physik*, 17, pp. 549–60 (1905).
209. M. Born in *Philosopher-Scientist*, p. 164.
210. *Ibid.*, p. 165.
211. *Inspiration of Science*, p. 24.
212. A. Einstein, *Annalen der Physik*, *17*, pp. 891–921 (1905).
213. *Philosopher-Scientist*, p. 49.
214. *Ibid.*, p. 53.
215. A. Einstein, *Annalen der Physik*, *14*, pp. 354–62 (1904).
216. *Philosopher-Scientist*, p. 21 and *A Centenary Volume*, pp. 265f. See also *Thematic Origins*, pp. 219–259.
217. *Ideas and Opinions*, p. 259.
218. *Ibid.*, p. 248.
219. *My generation*, p. 103.
220. *Ibid.*, p. 104.
221. *Philosopher-Scientist*, pp. 55f.
222. N. Bohr, *Atomic Theory and the Description of Nature*, NEW YORK: A.M.S. Press, 1978, p. 3.
223. *Ibid.*, p. 2.
224. *Philosopher-Scientist*, p. 57.
225. H. A. Lorentz, *Kon. Akademie van Wetenshappen Amsterdam*, *6*, pp. 809–31 (1904), (English edition).
226. *Thematic Origins*, pp. 169f.
227. *Later Years*, pp. 55f. See also *Ideas and Opinions*, p. 229 and *Philosopher-Scientist*, p. 55.

228. A. Einstein, quoted in *My generation*, p. 104.
229. A. Einstein, *Annalen der Physik, 18*, pp. 639–41 (1905).
230. A. Einstein, *Principle of Relativity*, p. 71.
231. *Thematic Origins*, p. 212.
232. R. W. Clark, *Einstein: The Life and Times*, NEW YORK and CLEVELAND: The World Publishing Company, 1971, pp. 59f.
233. Barbara L. Cline, *The Questioners: physicists and quantum theory*, NEW YORK: Thomas Y. Crowell, 1965, p. 83.
234. *Ibid.*, p. 60.
235. A. Einstein, quoted in *Life and Times*, p. 95.
236. *Ideas and Opinions*, p. 246.
237. *My generation*, pp. 18, 21 and 29.
238. *Ibid.*, p. 77.
239. *Assumption and Myth*, p. 56.
240. *Thematic Origins*, p. 394.
241. *Ibid.*, p. 170.
242. M. Born in *Philosopher-Scientist*, p. 168.
243. *The Questioners*, pp. 8–13.
244. *Ideas and Opinions*, p. 271.
245. *Ibid.*, pp. 42f.
246. *Ibid.*, p. 39.
247. *Ibid.*, p. 38.
248. *Ibid.*, p. 45.
249. A. Baker in *Random Walk*, p. 202.
250. *Ideas and Opinions*, p. 253.
251. *Ibid.*, p. 254.
252. *Philosopher-Scientist*, p. 23.
253. *Ideas and Opinions*, p. 255.
254. *Ibid.*, p. 256.
255. *Ibid.*, p. 257.
256. *Ibid.*, p. 23.
257. *Ibid.*, p. 258.
258. *Ibid.*, p. 260.
259. *Ibid.*, p. 261.
260. *Born-Einstein Letters*, p. 163.
261. *Ibid.*, p. 82.
262. T. S. Kuhn in *Criticism and the Growth of Knowledge*, CAMBRIDGE: Cambridge University Press, 1970, p. 1.
263. *Thematic Origins*, p. 471.
264. J. R. Oppenheimer, quoted in *The Questioners*, p. 126.
265. W. von Braun in *Random Walk*, p. 41.
266. *Ideas and Opinions*, p. 55.
267. *On Being Rational*, p. 247.
268. *Thematic Origins*, p. 179.
269. A. Einstein, quoted by M. Born in *Philosopher-Scientist*, p. 175.
270. *Later Years*, p. 59. See also *Ideas and Opinions*, p. 23.
271. *Science, Faith and Society*, pp. 34f.

272. *Ideas and Opinions*, pp. 277 and 23.
273. *Atomic Theory*, p. 1.
274. *Assumption and Myth*, p. 14.
275. *Ideas and Opinions*, pp. 276f.
276. A. Einstein, quoted in *Life and Times*, p. 10.
277. *Ideas and Opinions*, p. 14.
278. *Thematic Origins*, p. 457.
279. *The Questioners*, p. 46.
280. *Evolution of Physics*, p. 13.
281. M. Polanyi, *Personal Knowledge: Towards a Post-Critical Philosophy*, CHICAGO: University of Chicago Press, 1958, p. 286.
282. *Ideas and Opinions*, p. 324.
283. *Ibid.*, p. 20.
284. *My generation*, p. 2.
285. *Ibid.*, p. 67.
286. A. Einstein, quoted by G. Holton in *A Centenary Volume*, p. 161. See original source, *Later Years*, p. 61 where Einstein explained that by "comprehensibility" he meant the production of some sort of order among sense impressions.
287. Or a bubble chamber. See D. A. Glaser in *Random Walk*, p. 48.
288. *Later Years*, p. 124.
289. A. Einstein, quoted in *Thematic Origins*, p. 366.
290. *Personal Knowledge*, p. 329.
291. *Imagination and Growth*, pp. 2f.
292. *My generation*, pp. 65 and 152f.
293. A. Einstein, quoted in *Life and Times*, p. 131.
294. *My generation*, p. 68. See also *Imagination and Growth*, p. 4.
295. *Ideas and Opinions*, p. 4.
296. *Thematic Origins*, p. 374.
297. R. Bultmann, *Jesus Christ and Mythology*, NEW YORK: Charles Scribner's Sons, 1958, p. 83.
298. *Ibid.*, p. 35.
299. *Ibid.*, p. 18.
300. *Ibid.*, p. 38.
301. *Ibid.*, p. 20.
302. *Ibid.*, p. 66.
303. *Ibid.*, p. 19.
304. *Ibid.*, p. 25.
305. *Ibid.*, p. 42.
306. *Ibid.*, p. 39.
307. *Later Years*, pp. 59-64.
308. *Assumption and Myth*, p. 5.
309. *Science, Faith and Society*, pp. 63f.
310. *Ideas and Opinions*, p. 50.
311. *Mythology*, p. 40.
312. *Ibid.*, p. 65.
313. *Ibid.*, p. 41.

314. *Ibid.*, p. 36.
315. *Ibid.*, p. 37.
316. *A Centenary Volume*, pp. 310f.
317. *Mythology*, p. 27.
318. *Ibid.*, p. 21.
319. *Ibid.*, p. 14.
320. L. L. Whyte in *Einstein: the man*, pp. 56f.
321. M. Planck, *Deutsche physikalische Gesellschaft, 2*, p. 202 (1900).
322. M. Klein in *A Centenary Volume*, p. 140.
323. M. Planck, quoted in *Thematic Origins*, p. 215.
324. A. Einstein, *Annalen der Physik, 9*, p. 417 (1902).
325. J. H. Poincaré, *Bull. Sci. Math., 28*, p. 302 (1904).
326. J. H. Poincaré, *Com. rend. Acad. Sci., 140*, p. 1504 (1905).
327. H. Bondi, *Relativity and Common Sense*, LONDON: Heinemann, 1965, p. 58.
328. H. A. Lorentz in *Principle of Relativity*, pp. 12f.
329. *Thematic Origins*, p. 205.
330. A. Einstein, quoted in *Thematic Origins*, p. 229.
331. *Creator and Rebel*, p. 78.
332. *Ideas and Opinions*, p. 247.
333. Ilse Rosenthal-Schneider, quoted in *Thematic Origins*, pp. 236f.
334. *Later Years*, p. 83f.
335. *Philosopher-Scientist*, pp. 7–13.
336. G. J. Whitrow in *Einstein: the man*, p. 11.
337. *Ibid.*, p. 12.
338. *Philosopher-Scientist*, p. 29 and *Ideas and Opinions*, p. 248.
339. A. Einstein in *Principle of Relativity*, pp. 35–65.
340. H. Minkowski in *Principle of Relativity*, p. 75.
341. *Ideas and Opinions*, pp. 233–5.
342. H. Minkowski in *Principle of Relativity*, p. 41.
343. *Special and General Theories*, p. 57 and *Philosopher-Scientist*, p. 59.
344. G. J. Whitrow in *Einstein: the man*, p. 5.
345. *Philosopher-Scientist*, p. 67.
346. *Ideas and Opinions*, pp. 288f.
347. *The Human Side*, pp. 67f.
348. *Creator and Rebel*, pp. 123f.
349. *Ideas and Opinions*, p. 80.
350. *Philosopher-Scientist*, p. 3.
351. A. Einstein, *The World as I See It*, translated A. Harris, NEW YORK: Citadel Press, 1979, p. 5.
352. *Ideas and Opinions*, p. 46f.
353. *Philosopher-Scientist*, pp. 4f.
354. *Ideas and Opinions*, p. 43.
355. *Ibid.*, p. 337.
356. *As I See It*, pp. 111f.
357. *Later Years*, p. 83.
358. O. Frisch in *Einstein: the man*, p. 31.

359. *Ideas and Opinions*, p. 233.
360. *A Centenary Volume*, pp. 312f.
361. *Assumption and Myth*, p. 8.
362. *Evolution of Physics*, p. 4.
363. *Ibid.*, p. 10.
364. *Philosopher-Scientist*, pp. 683f and *Ideas and Opinions*, p. 19.
365. F. S. C. Northrop in *Albert Einstein, Philosopher-Scientist*, p. 388.
366. *Later Years*, p. 32.
367. *Assumption and Myth*, p. 10.
368. *Ibid.*, p. 11.

AUTHOR INDEX

SUBJECT INDEX

refinement, 96f.
refutability, 9, 44, 45, 78, 108
relation, science to theology, 8, 12, 22
    scientist to God, 56f.
relativism, 70, 76
religion, religious, 2, 6, 11, 23, 57, 77, 92, 122, 123, 124, 125
reorientation, 53, 75, 83
repeatability, 29
revelation, 77, 87, 124, 125
revolution, scientific, 17, 53, 63, 73, 113

Saviour, 129
scepticism, 131
scientific research, role of, 5f.
scientific researcher, 25–31
scientific thinking, 13, 17ff.
Scripture, 103f.
Second Law of Thermodynamics, 68f., 111
security, 31, 56
simultaneity, 70, 81, 82, 84, 116, 117, 122
social responsibility, 23, 24, 25, 26, 27, 28, 30, 93, 99f., 101, 103
special theory of relativity, 6, 15, 21, 32, 40, 44, 46, 47, 53, 62, 68ff., 72, 73, 82, 83f., 112, 113, 114, 115f., 118, 119, 121f.
speculation, 24, 30, 61, 92, 94, 113, 122, 126
statistical mechanics, 67, 111
stereochemistry, 63
subjectivity, 24, 37, 63, 77, 92, 99, 107, 123
suffering, 88

Talents, 8, 9, 10
technological, 7f., 9, 12, 24, 99, 100, 101, 102, 103
technologists, 2, 8f., 23, 88, 98, 107, 109
technology, 3, 4f., 61, 88, 92f., 94, 100, 102, 103, 105, 106, 107, 108, 109, 129
theologian, 19, 88, 94
theology, theological, 1, 2, 3, 9, 10, 12, 13, 57f., 59, 61f., 77, 88, 91, 92, 98, 109, 122, 123, 125, 129, 130
theories, scientific, 17f., 19, 35, 37–40, 47, 76, 126f., 129, 130, 131
theory-laden, 33, 44, 74, 99
time dilation, 71
truth, 15, 16, 18ff., 37, 40, 41, 44, 45, 55, 77, 108, 119, 126, 127, 129
truth-content, 19, 39, 54f.

Unspecifiability, 22, 46f., 49, 75

Validity, valid, 17, 18, 23, 34, 39, 48, 49, 54, 58, 91, 94, 95, 104, 107, 109, 123, 124
vocation, vocational, 1, 22, 27, 29, 31, 99, 101

Wave-particle duality, 65f., 67, 69
wisdom, scientific, 2, 45, 57, 59, 61, 75, 78, 81, 88, 131
world-view, 103f., 105, 106, 107, 108
Word of God, 57, 59, 87, 103